# ACCELERATE!

Every owner of a physical copy of this edition of

# *ACCELERATE!*

can download the eBook for free direct from us at Harriman House, in a DRM-free format that can be read on any eReader, tablet or smartphone.

Simply head to:

**ebooks.harriman-house.com/accelerate**

to get your copy now.

# ACCELERATE!

The essential guide to growing
your trades businesss

**Dan Matthews**

Foreword by **Richard Harpin**

HARRIMAN HOUSE LTD
18 College Street
Petersfield
Hampshire
GU31 4AD
GREAT BRITAIN
Tel: +44 (0)1730 233870

Email: enquiries@harriman-house.com
Website: www.harriman-house.com

First published in Great Britain in 2018.
Copyright © Checkatrade

The right of Dan Matthews to be identified as the Author has been asserted in accordance with the Copyright, Design and Patents Act 1988.

Paperback ISBN: 978-0-85719-728-3
eBook ISBN: 978-0-85719-729-0

British Library Cataloguing in Publication Data
A CIP catalogue record for this book can be obtained from the British Library.

**Hh** Harriman House

# CONTENTS

## 5. Getting the Most Out of Technology and Systems 73

## 6. Taking on Employees and Building Your Team  87

## 7. Dealing with Money  107

## 8. Keeping on Top of Legal Stuff  129

# FOREWORD BY RICHARD HARPIN

O ver the last 25 years I have been lucky enough to build HomeServe from a loss-making plumbing and heating business called FastFix, based in Newcastle-upon-Tyne, into a global business worth over £3 billion with 8.4 million customers, 6,000 staff and EBITDA profit approaching £200m.

Now I want to help a million trades across 15 countries to grow their business in a digital world where the pace of change is moving faster and faster. Had I been starting out today I think it would have been much more difficult. How can small firms and one-person trades businesses compete with Amazon and Google?

That's why we acquired Checkatrade, the UK market leader in providing home improvement and repair work to local trades and helping them build an online profile and reputation. Already we have set up a buying club to pass on discounts on fuel, insurance, vehicles, materials and much more to our members. Next, we will be offering free software to help trades run their businesses more effectively, followed by a better way to get emergency jobs to you, an apprentice programme and online training courses.

I commissioned this book in the hope that you will be able to pick up one or two ideas of what has worked for other successful businesses, and then go on to apply those ideas in your own.

I wish you every success in the world as you grow your business. Do please let me know how you get on and what works for you so that we can share it with others.

**Richard Harpin**
*Founder and Chief Executive, HomeServe plc*
*Chairman, Checkatrade*

# INTRODUCTION

The trades economy in the UK is huge – adding billions of pounds to GDP and with millions of people working in it. It has, of course, been around for ages – after all, people throughout history have learned trades and performed services in return for money. But there's probably never been a more exciting time to be part of it.

Why?

Because the limits on how fast and how far you can take your trades business are disappearing. Thanks to digital innovations such as Checkatrade, anyone working in a trade today has a golden opportunity to scale up and create a sizeable – and immensely profitable – business.

It's a huge generational leap.

With the help of technology, you can truly stand apart – with spot-on branding, marketing and slick operations, giving confidence to legions of customers up and down the country. Good work speaks volumes – and to a wider audience than ever before. Meanwhile, you can be in complete control of your finances, team, strategy, and more – usually at the touch of a button (or tap of a smartphone screen), giving you the fuel you need to do an efficient, professional job every time.

And you can be any kind of trades business.

And your business can be any size.

Plumbing, electrical services, roofing, locksmithing, gardening, landscaping, painting and decorating, and kitchen-fitting... The opportunities are endless and hugely exciting.

This book is all about unlocking them for you.

There's no unique 'type' of person that can grow a business like this. It doesn't require an elusive gift for commerce or particularly special (or secret) knowledge. Quite a few tradespeople think that growing a business is beyond their skillset. But the truth is that anyone can grasp the basics of good service, team-building, marketing and money – and create something truly special.

This book will prove this to you.

It will give you the business skillset you need. And, perhaps just as important, the mindset. We will look at the fundamentals of growth, including marketing techniques for online and offline, tactics to build a workforce without putting a strain on cash flow, borrowing to invest, and developing a sophisticated sales strategy – all while fulfilling your legal and financial obligations.

Even more importantly, we will look at real-life stories of tradespeople just like you – with businesses at every stage of development. They share their no-nonsense advice and hard-earned wisdom so that anyone can follow in their footsteps.

Most tradespeople work on their own, perhaps engaging subcontractors or casual labour when necessary. But by focusing on growth you can employ talented recruits, increase revenue, expand territorially and become more successful than you possibly could working alone. As many of the tradespeople in this book will attest, it can be an amazingly fulfilling experience quite apart from the financial rewards.

It's time to accelerate!

# CHAPTER
# ONE

*The Secrets of Success*

"By the time you've finished this book, you should be equipped with everything you need."

**S**uccess comes in many shapes and sizes. For inspiration, here are three very different stories from tradespeople who have reached the top – all in their own unique way.

By the time you've finished this book, you should be equipped with everything you need to make your own journey to success – whatever that looks like for you.

# CHARLIE MULLINS,
## Pimlico Plumbers

Charlie Mullins is probably the UK's most famous plumber. Though his business is based in and around the capital, having expanded from its roots in south east London, his successful PR campaigns have given the business international fame.

"My target is to get to £100m turnover," he explains. "We're at £40m now. I've always been a bit dubious about extending outside the M25 but the way we are growing it's going to happen. There's still a lot of work in London and we need to sew up a bit more of the market share here before we move out.

"Because of the PR we're getting requests all the time to open up in Scotland, Birmingham, Manchester – even Abu Dhabi and Dubai. I would say we're the most recognisable plumbing business in the world."

Today he oversees 430 staff and more than 250 vans, but like many tradespeople, Charlie started his career as an apprentice. He believes this is the best way into the plumbing industry because you get paid to learn. He was diligent in those early years as a fresh-faced teenager. As a result, when his apprenticeship was over, many customers stuck with him as he launched his own business.

He started doing jobs in the Sidcup area, but his company's first big break came when he adopted the name 'Pimlico', a move inspired by local estate agents who had earned an upmarket reputation by incorporating a reference to that well-heeled part of London in their own name.

The business's new premium brand, coupled with its founder's commitment to high standards, gradually earned more customers, an effect magnified by word-of-mouth recommendations. This was a time – the early 1980s – when service did not come as standard and charlatans were everywhere, so people were looking for good experiences.

"It's obvious when you think about it," says Charlie. "It's a personal service with someone you don't know coming into your house. It makes a big difference if they are polite, smartly dressed and can communicate properly – back then none of that was guaranteed.

"That's how I approached the job starting out and, when I started recruiting people, I expected them to do the same. It might sound stupid now, but that's why we became successful in the early days, just getting the basics right like explaining things clearly and tidying up after ourselves."

After more than 40 years in the business, Pimlico Plumbers now occupies a 30,000 sq ft HQ and a number of railway arches in Lambeth. The building houses the management, call centre staff, IT people, operations, PR, caterers and vehicle mechanics.

The team moved into it in 2000, having grown out of a 5,000 sq ft space down the road. Solving an overcrowding problem by moving into premises six times bigger might seem like overkill, but Charlie says it represented another turning point – so much so that 18 years later he's looking to acquire more land and additional premises to accommodate the booming business.

"When we first moved in I wondered what we would do with all the space and how we'd fill it. But that was a big step forwards because it gave us the opportunity to expand – as opposed to expanding and then having to find the space. It meant we could do more and take on different types of work.

"We had moved from somewhere much smaller and it gave us impetus to make Pimlico Plumbers into a bigger business. I did plan to rent some space out at the start and I never thought we'd outgrow it, but we have now."

The business developed its customer base and moved beyond plumbing to becoming a more complete service provider: "We stepped it up to take in other trades, like roofing, carpentry, electrics, tiling, painting and appliances. We became a more rounded company and it created extra work."

Yet another impetus – one which Charlie credits with driving the business into the big time and helping it become one of London's most recognisable brands – is public relations and marketing. Pimlico Plumbers has enjoyed exposure on diverse media platforms, from primetime news to talent shows.

The foray into PR started by chance, but today the business is on a permanent charm offensive to spread the word.

"We commissioned some electric shutters for the new office in about 2001," Charlie remembers. "The company supplying them were based up north and the manager came down to check on the work. He asked if he could do a few pictures and they'd do some PR on it – I honestly didn't know what he meant.

"He said it was good for them to say they were down in London working. A PR guy came down to help, I thought he was clued-up and he asked who did our PR – again I didn't really understand what he meant. He gave me their number, we're still with them today, a company called Recognition.

"It amazes me that I didn't see it, but now I can't believe anyone can get by without it. The PR took us to a different level. In business you can be the best in London but if people don't know about you there's no point. We had a nice steady business, a good business that operated within a few miles of Pimlico where people knew us, but outside of that no one did.

"You can't do without it, even if you do it yourself. It's a bit like asking if you can have a business without a website – of course you can't."

The PR attack is reinforced in the real world by a clean image which has endured since the early days, despite the expansion of the business and its hundreds of employees. Its staff of plumbers drive well-equipped Volkswagen Transporter vans with distinctive livery and a trademark (usually amusing) personalised number plate.

This all adds up to strong brand collateral and a high level of trust and loyalty among the customer base. Charlie admits that his 'clean' approach is much more common than it was when he started, so new elements such as technology (engineers carry iPads instead of paper and pens) serve to create a point of difference.

TV helped to clean up the industry, with programmes outing dodgy dealers and forcing others to clean up their act, while at the same time showing viewers what a job well done looks like. People won't put up with what they did 20 years ago and fewer are vulnerable to getting ripped off because of online feedback and review services like Checkatrade.

According to Charlie, the opportunities for growth are coming thick and fast, which makes recruitment easier than it used to be. But although his eyes are fixed on the future, he refuses to neglect the company's legion of devoted customers.

"The longer you stay in business and the more success you experience, the further your reputation will travel. We're doing 2,500 jobs a week and 75% of those are customers who have used us before. It's a big base of returning customers. They wouldn't ring us back if they couldn't trust us.

"Recruitment is easier now because it's a nice big headquarters, they are full-time now, people get training and they get the uniform and the nice van. It's not hard to recruit when you can offer that – the only tough bit is taking five to interview and only one gets the job. We pay the best so we can pick the best.

"When I started out being professional was quite rare and it was the secret of my early success so that's very important to me. As the business grows we have maintained that by taking on more quality control managers. We have been around nearly 40 years, so anyone who comes on board knows what we expect from them."

He adds: "We have a bigger call centre, we have more office space and business is looking great. We're spreading out geographically, right up to the M25 now, throughout Greater London and getting into some of the areas we didn't cover so much before like Richmond, Barnes, Bromley, and Kingston."

Kingston to Abu Dhabi is admittedly a major leap, but if there's one trades business that can bridge the gap it's Pimlico Plumbers. Its masterly use of media channels, coupled with its tight focus on customer service and quality work means this business has the chance to go global.

"There's plenty of scope to grow," says Charlie. "But we don't want to overstretch ourselves at the expense of doing good quality work. We'll keep on expanding at our own pace, making sure that customers are happy wherever they are."

# WAYNE DE WET,
## *Wayne de Wet Painting and Decorating Services*

Professional painter and decorator Wayne de Wet has DIY in his blood. Some of his early memories are of assisting his "hands-on" dad doing jobs around the house. These included gas and electric repairs, carpentry, tiling and carpet fitting; projects which taught him both the right and the wrong way to go about working as a tradesman.

"My dad was an avid DIYer and obviously I became his assistant, so I got into it from an early age," says Wayne. "He was fearless and good with his hands, but when I grew up it was a pleasure to teach him a thing or two in return. I'd say 'Dad, did you know you're not supposed to plaster over hardboard?'

"My uncle used to run a banger racing club in Essex. They would strip down the cars and we would paint them in bright colours and creative patterns. It was fun to be around paint. These two experiences in my early life meant I was destined to become a painter and decorator."

It was during these tender years that Wayne developed an obsession with what he calls "doing things properly" and "going the extra mile". Throughout his career he has worked to be better than the rest and today he is one of the most in-demand tradespeople in his county.

He resisted the temptation to recruit and has remained a sole trader. The reason he gives is that customers have always wanted to book him personally and seek assurances that his hands, not those of an employee, will carry out the work.

With good reason. Wayne is a stickler for detail and gets a lot of personal satisfaction from surpassing customer expectations.

"I have created a niche market where everyone gets what they want, whatever their whim. No matter how fussy they are, I will accommodate them," he explains.

"I have numerous examples of this. In one case I painted and wallpapered an entire house in accordance with a specification from a designer. I hung all the paper and decorated the rooms, then the customer came back, said they had changed their mind and wanted the paper in the lounge to be put up in the hall.

"They were happy with the job and the quality of the work, but they wanted a change. I said 'no problem', took it all down and did it again. You get paid again, the customer is happy, you get a recommendation – so being patient like this is a real plus."

Clients like these become his chief ambassadors, a sort of unofficial sales team. They talk up his work at the office or during parties and the focus is often on the things he does differently. It might be the fact he takes his shoes off or cleans as he goes, but the details count.

"It's little things like ensuring paint doesn't go on plug sockets. I've repainted walls before where the last painter didn't bother, so I scrubbed off the old paint and the look is so much better. It's going the extra mile. In general, I let the customer engage me and I draw from them the expectations about the job. When I first arrive it's important to get into their thoughts and understand the little niggles they have.

"A typical one is coving around the ceiling, the joins are usually disgusting. I'll ask if they want me to make these little annoyances disappear. They are pleasantly surprised. So my advice is engage the customer, get into their heads and exceed their expectations while keeping the costs under control."

There are other trade secrets too. Wayne regularly asks customers' permission to film the room he's about to start working in. The reason for this 'before' shot is not to contrast it with an 'after' shot, but to serve as a memory aid when it comes to putting the room back together when he is finished.

Painting and decorating usually requires moving pictures, mirrors, furniture and ornaments. The film shows where each item is supposed to be placed back.

> "Clients are excited when they come back from holiday to see the room is decorated to a really high standard; it's clean, hoovered and everything is back exactly where it was. That sort of experience travels and they become your ambassador."

The approach has earned Wayne a high-quality customer base and a pipeline of work that's limited only by his refusal to take on too much. He estimates he turns down 60% of enquiries and even the jobs he accepts aren't penned into the diary until his current work is completed to everyone's satisfaction.

He says: "Once the customer has signed the paperwork and paid a small refundable booking deposit, they secure a pencil date in the diary. It's not penned in because until I finish the job I'm on, the next job needs to wait. Nine times out of ten the customer will ask for something extra, such as putting up a new curtain rail or pictures.

> "Love the customer you are with. They are your most important customer – so give them all of your attention. Don't rush to the next one. I tell the next one the approximate date I can start and firm it up two or three days before finishing the current job."

With decades of experience in the bag, Wayne knows the projects he likes. Generally speaking, he doesn't do exteriors because the British weather too often causes delay and disruption to jobs, which in turn puts pressure on cash flow.

Taking a formal, professional and detailed approach also gives Wayne the opportunity to be firm when it comes to money. He's not shy about quoting a fee and expects to be paid on time. He has devoted time and energy to the job and he's committed to a high-quality finish, so he expects customers to respect his business in return.

To smooth the process, he makes his approach to payments clear during the consultation stage. Introducing money talk early avoids confusion – and perhaps confrontation – later on.

> "I'm always managing expectations of work, cost and timings. I'm not shy to talk about money, I go to work to earn a living. At the end of the consultation I talk about it and explain how the business works – if I work for four weeks I will invoice every week and I will expect to be paid.

> "When a garage services your car it holds on to it until you pay, it doesn't invoice and wait 30 days. Tradespeople should be no different. I'm a small business and I need to pay my bills, so when I've done the work I expect to be paid. If there is an issue I expect customers to engage with me about it."

He isn't short of bookings, but Wayne still uses a range of platforms to keep people talking about his business. Twenty-five years ago most trades people relied on word-of-mouth for work, which remains a solid way to develop new business. But today online services like Checkatrade provide an opportunity to amplify the effect. Before, customers would share information with friends and family, so the impact was local. Online, the ripples go a lot further.

"These days, would you go on holiday without checking TripAdvisor or a review site for your hotel? Or go to a restaurant without looking online for people's experiences of the food and service?" asks Wayne.

"Checkatrade shows everything including pictures, qualifications, insurance, skills and previous jobs. Everything is checked, verified and shown on your profile. It's changed the way work comes to me – it's a whole new customer base on top of what I had before."

He has a suite of social media profiles, with a presence on Twitter, Facebook and YouTube. He has also become known as a tester, promotor and even distributor of cutting-edge new products in the painting and decorating market – all of which helps to solidify the name de Wet as a trailblazer in the profession.

> "I've always been incredibly nosy and I've always wanted to know what is the latest paint, latest tools and best brushes. I've essentially become an industry expert testing and reviewing products.

> "I've created a college roadshow where I give away tools from the brands. I take video and images of the youngsters using the tools and I share that across social media. I write content about it as Wayne de Wet, the consultant product tester."

His experience of the industry means he can push good products into new markets: "Four years ago I wrote to an American company to send me some samples of some products I wanted to write a review about. They sent them over and I loved them, so I wrote two reviews, but they followed up and said I couldn't do that because they aren't available in the UK.

> "I offered to introduce them to a UK distributor and help get the products into the UK. Now another part of what I do is help good products into market. I do it with brands from the US, UK and further afield.

> "I also do consultancy and testing, giving them instant feedback to take back into the laboratory and perfect the product. Last year I helped to design a pair of painters' trousers."

Marketing, then, isn't an issue for Wayne. He has one eye on life in retirement, as he admits that his trade takes its toll on the body.

Developing industry expertise beyond applying paint and paper to walls is smoothing that transition, while bringing him additional profile as a go-to source of advice.

By diversifying and finding new revenue channels, he plans to continue earning a living and commanding the respect of his peers long after he hangs up his brushes for good.

# DAVE GREEN,
## Wesson Fencing

In 2008, Wesson Fencing was on its knees and about to go out of business when Dave Green, an entrepreneur with no experience of fencing or landscaping, decided to buy it out of receivership for £25,000.

His background was in vehicle crash repair and he was more comfortable with panel-beating than grounds maintenance, but he wanted a change of direction and believed that working in the fresh air was the way forward.

With the help of five existing staff, plus some new recruits, he rejuvenated the business and within a few years had turned it into one of the sector's main contractors in the Surrey area. Its strong reputation has won it major contracts in the private sector as well as local authorities, schools and community centres.

Dave remembers: "When I took over the business I immediately looked at the order book and accounts; there was a lot of unpaid debt and clearing that was an early focus. Although it was in trouble, I kept the name Wesson Fencing because the company had been trading for nearly 50 years and was well-known in the area. But, nevertheless, it had been let go.

"I reassured the staff that we would build the business up, not that I had any experience in fencing at all. But first I had to lay off staff who were not willing to work a full day, because they were so used to going home early.

"The core staff stayed and are here still. We've had others come and go; even today it's difficult to get staff for this industry. We advertise on **www.gov.uk/jobsearch** and elsewhere online. Fencing is a niche market so it's tough but we always seem to get there."

Another key issue was rebuilding trust in the supply chain. Wesson had bad debts and despite new ownership, previous suppliers washed their hands of the company. Desperate for materials, Dave found three suppliers prepared to risk a new relationship with the endangered business.

"I still use them today. As they helped me when I needed them, I will not go anywhere else. My two biggest suppliers of timber and panels deal on trust. I have never filled in an account form with either of them – that's well over £150,000 of business per year."

Having restructured the core business and cut out dead wood, Dave looked for opportunities to advertise Wesson's services and take on new customers.

"That's when I met Kevin Byrne. He was just in the process of setting up Checkatrade, which I saw as a good idea and probably the best form of advertising. So I signed up for a number of their directories – we now appear in around six.

"Appearing on the Checkatrade website is definitely the best form of advertising; even now when I ask customers where they got our details, it's always Checkatrade. We create sales through our good reputation and it helps to spread the word. We have very few complaints or call-backs; I'm very proud of this because it's hard work to maintain a good reputation."

As well as signing up early with Checkatrade, Dave contacted nearby schools and local authorities, which quickly became among the business's biggest customers. Schools would refer other schools and the holiday periods became extremely busy for Wesson.

It was the same story with councils. Dave emailed them and secured jobs to replace old or damaged fences. The business soon developed a reputation for no-nonsense, high-quality work and for "just getting the job done".

To support the growing sales inventory, the business took on an accountant and bought a licence with a smart online accounting system. Then an admin assistant was brought in to chase payments and collect money owed.

Careful not to make things too high-tech, the old whiteboard was thrown out and replaced with a T-Card system, which provided a visual list of booked work and live jobs. It helped the team manage workflow and understand what was needed to complete each task.

As the business grew, operations were formalised. Wesson hired another admin assistant with responsibility for health and safety compliance and risk assessments. The business signed up to official training programmes in which staff learned important aspects of the law. Recently it even published a privacy policy in line with new legislation – quite a departure from the shabby systems in place when Dave bought the company from receivership.

But even as the business righted itself and began to do well, all wasn't plain sailing: "Around three years ago we had to find new premises as our current yard was being flattened to make way for housing. Though that was pretty daunting it was probably for the best.

"I took the decision to purchase a shop in the local high street, which has proved a real asset: we get our name out there, passing traffic and footfall have helped to build the business further.

"I also found a much larger yard to rent. It has been invaluable, because the amount of business we have now means our previous yard would have been far too small. We have increased our vehicle fleet, our staff numbers and our sales. It hasn't been easy but I'm positive that things can only get better; hard work and determination has taken our business from near-collapse to success."

Dave has lots of advice to his fellow tradespeople, ranging from getting the basics right and responding to queries in a timely manner, to resolving issues fast to make sure customers are left feeling happy and well cared for.

He thinks honesty is important too: "Be honest if you are too busy to quote or have a full order book. Tell the customer, because most are prepared to wait if they are given a firm date in the future."

Following simple rules like these helped Wesson out of receivership, through tentative steps towards growth and into robust, stable territory. Before Dave took over the business, its best sales year was £325,0000. In his first year in charge it hit half a million in sales, which soon grew close to a million.

If he can achieve this level of success with a business with a bad reputation going in reverse, imagine what you can do from square one – with solid foundations and a good reputation.

# CHAPTER TWO

*Getting Your Name
Out There*

You might have a fantastic business with brilliant customer service, a team of skilled people and a price list that undercuts the competition. But if no one knows about it then none of this matters. Having a good business but no customers is a bit like staging the FA Cup final without selling any tickets.

Yet, sadly, the best tradespeople aren't always the best marketers, which means they miss out on top jobs to others who might be less qualified but are better at boasting. If you fit into the former category, it's time to make some changes.

Setting aside a few hours each week to work on marketing can pay dividends, literally. It could lead to a deluge of new jobs, or a refined selection of higher-paid ones which prise open profit margins without lumping on additional cost.

Whatever your goals, marketing is a brilliant way to build a business fast. The good news is that there are plenty of ways to spread the word, so you can pick and choose the mix that suits you best.

"Sign-writing, work shirts with logos and branded communication all help to reinforce the image of our company."

– *Chris Fairbairn, Cribbit Installations Ltd*

In this chapter we'll look at the good old-fashioned stuff you can do without a computer. Of course, the internet influences everything these days, but a blend of on- and offline channels will deliver the biggest rewards.

The key is to experiment. Don't try and do everything at once. As you know, it's better to do a few jobs well than to try and do too many half-heartedly.

Do a marketing drive, gauge the results, then try something new. By discovering what works best you'll improve efficiency and drive down waste. It's a great way to find out what gives your business the best bang for its buck.

# BRANDING

Think of two airlines, easyJet and British Airways. They essentially offer the same service: to fly you from one place to another. The businesses are the same, broadly speaking, but the identities are completely different. BA is premium. It wants you to relax and enjoy the ride in comfort, peace of mind and, some would say, in style. Flights are more expensive in many cases, but you're paying for extra service.

Then there's easyJet: it wants to get you from point A to point B with the minimum amount of cost and fuss. It's not luxurious, but it is cheap and no-nonsense.

The important point is that neither of these airlines is better than the other. They simply target different parts of the same market. Their respective brands tell the customer which is which.

> "If you get the chance to correct something that a previous tradesperson has done badly, then grab it. In my case they might have neglected to clean paint off plug sockets or something else that looks sloppy. I cut around the sockets, but I also clean off the old paint so that my job looks extra professional, especially compared to the last one. It adds to my brand as someone who cares about a first-class finish."

**– Wayne de Wet, Wayne de Wet Painting and Decorating Services**

You can imagine a brand as the foundations that all other types of marketing sit on. It's a description (visual, written and experiential) of who you are and, just as importantly, how you want to come across to prospective customers. A good brand is consistent and influences everything from uniforms to the way you treat people.

Branding matters because it's the first sign of what your business is. It tells people whether you are premium or low-cost, cutting edge or traditional, customer-centric or focused on efficiency. People make decisions fast and first impressions count, so ensure your branding conveys the message you want it to.

> "I love my design on my van. It's 'wicked', to quote a customer. It's clear, different and memorable. I am also very proud that it is a product of my own imagination: my hand holding a paintbrush, showing precision.
>
> "The first seven years of my company I was working from my personal car, a red Mazda RX-8, with no branding. It was a smart car and I got clever at packing, plus I was very careful! But since investing in the van and sign-writing, it has been seen everywhere. 'I saw your van in the garden centre', 'I saw your van while I was shopping', 'Yes I have seen your van around' are some quotes from customers and trade companies in the area."

*– Jane Pennock, Us Girls Decorating Ltd*

Essentially, a brand consists of a few key elements:

- company name
- logo
- colour scheme

- consistent designs
- consistent messaging
- tagline
- behaviour
- communications.

To build a new brand, or develop an existing one, you have to ask yourself some questions, mainly about the nature of your business and the type of customer you want to attract. So:

- Who is your ideal customer?
- What characteristics do you want them to see in your business?
- Is your approach low-cost or high-end?
- What aspects could you promote? (For example, customer service or efficiency.)
- What is your ultimate objective: to grow big or stay relatively small?
- Generally, how do you want to be known?

Once you have the answers, you can start to build your brand. Use them to describe your business to a designer, who will create your branded materials, such as business cards, leaflets or a design for your vehicles. Alternatively, you can do this yourself with low-cost web tools.

Type 'logo design' into a search engine and you'll see a list of design businesses offering to create your logo. Many of these can also build a simple website, business cards, letterheads and envelopes as part of a relatively low-cost package – that means sub-£500.

But your brand is more than sharp designs and catchy colour schemes. It is effected by everything you do, including how you and your team approach a job from the moment a customer rings you to invoicing and aftercare.

Remember: to create a brand that people appreciate, you must be consistent in everything you do. It's no good setting up a 'prestige' landscaping business if the veneer of quality is ruined by bad language, tired, dirty clothing and missed appointments.

"We made sure that we had a name that is relevant to the trade – LSW *Decorating* instead of LSW Contracting. We also strive to do the best job possible, so that word of mouth can also work. We have t-shirts, business cards, paid ads online that appear near the top of Google, and advertisement boards when we work outside."

**LSW|DECORATING**

**– Chris Jones, LSW Decorating Ltd**

# PRINTED MARKETING

Once you have your brand – including a logo, colour scheme and agreed business principles – you can start putting it to work. A tried-and-tested method of doing this is distributing printed materials, such as leaflets, billboards and signs, or advertising in magazines and newspapers.

Spending on print has been challenged by digital advertising in the last decade or so – more on this later – but many people, particularly those not born into the internet era, appreciate the tangible feel of paper over online alternatives.

## Leaflet dropping

The number of leaflets and brochures that plop onto your doormat every morning illustrates that this method of reaching out is still as popular as ever. It also tells you that printed adverts are in competition with each other – so yours has to stand out from the pile.

As with business cards and letterheads, designing a leaflet can be cheap or pricey, depending on which route you take. This time, search for 'leaflet design printing UK' to see a list of services.

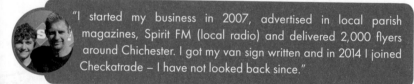

> "When I first set up, my wife and my then three-year-old son leafleted hundreds of properties with homemade flyers, which we created ourselves to save money. As we started to get calls, I had some posters made for local convenience stores and supermarkets. I left business cards at fish-and-chip shops and hairdressers."

*– Jordan Williams, JR Williams Plumbing Services Ltd*

Vistaprint, at the time of writing, lets you design your own message (incorporating your new brand designs, of course) and print 5,000 leaflets for under £45. A more luxury look and feel will set you back around £75. Hundreds of other services give you cheaper (or dearer) options.

So getting leaflets printed is relatively straightforward, but this still leaves the job of trudging round 5,000 addresses and hand-delivering your offers to residents, not all of whom will be happy to receive them.

It's important to weigh up the time this will take – you could employ a firm to do the deliveries for you or have them inserted into a local newspaper – and the negative side effects of irritating homeowners.

> "I started my business in 2007, advertised in local parish magazines, Spirit FM (local radio) and delivered 2,000 flyers around Chichester. I got my van sign written and in 2014 I joined Checkatrade – I have not looked back since."

*– Simon Pitham, SEP Tiling Ltd*

# SUCCESS STORIES ▐▐▐▐▌▶

**Name:** Simon Pitham
**Business name:** SEP Tiling
**Type of business:** Floor and wall tiling
**Number of employees:** 1 (apprentice)

### How did you get started in your trade?

"Eleven years ago, I was working as a produce shift manager and decided I needed a new challenge in life. I wanted a new career and to run my own business, so I booked myself onto a tiling course."

### Has the business changed since you started?

"The business has changed massively for me in a few ways, particularly with growth in the number of customers and repeat customers. This has helped me to take on an apprentice, which is very exciting."

### Describe your typical customer and project.

"My typical customers are private households in the domestic sector. We do bathrooms, conservatories, kitchens and so on. But to grow the business I now work in the commercial sector, tiling shops and showrooms, for example."

### What do you enjoy about your career?

"I enjoy meeting customers new and old, as well as the satisfaction of our work once it's finished."

(RIGHT) *Simon Pitham, pictured with his apprentice Harrison.*

**What's the hardest thing about it, or the biggest challenge you face?**

"The hardest thing about the work, I suppose, is how physical it can be at times, and the biggest challenge is to keep up with the amount of work coming in. There never seems to be enough hours in the day."

**What are your plans for the future?**

"My plans for the future are to keep up with the demand and grow the business even further, by taking on another apprentice once Harrison, my current apprentice, is fully trained."

**What's your best tip for other tradespeople in your sector?**

"Keep grafting and be happy!"

## Local press

If the above isn't for you, consider newspaper or magazine advertising. For this, you'll still need to design an advert, but you don't have to worry about distributing it as the publication itself takes care of the legwork.

Like in the case of leaflet-dropping, it's a scatter-gun approach: you hit a lot of potential customers and hope a small proportion will notice your ad and pick up the phone. Whether your campaign is a success or not comes down to the value of your new customers and whether it represents an increase on what you had before, after time and costs are factored in.

Advertising in the printed press, even a small local publication, will add some costs – how much depends on the size, prestige and circulation of the publication you want to be included in. A parish journal or local guide might only be £50–£100. But a regional newspaper could be ten times that figure or more. Ask to see proof of success before you spend that sort of money.

What you are paying for is an audience that you couldn't hope to reach on your own. Plus, there's the 'prestige' of being associated with a respected professional publication – this can add weight to your business.

# OUTDOOR DISPLAY

Not everyone loves being targeted by advertisers in their own home. Most leaflets go straight in the bin and only a handful are acted on immediately or tucked away behind the fruit bowl for future reference.

Also, you might not relish the thought of tiptoeing up garden paths to drop a marketing message on an unsuspecting stranger. So you might want to consider something called 'outdoor media' – i.e. posters, billboards and signs.

Years ago, advertising had its time and place. When the architect Albert Moore rebuilt what we now know as London's OXO Tower in the late 1920s, he managed to wrong-foot regulators by incorporating the brand name in the building's giant windows. This was despite a city-wide ban on skyline advertising – and it still stands today, proudly defying the law.

In this day and age, display advertising is not only allowed but expected just about everywhere, from roundabouts to fuel pumps to crop circles. If there's a square metre of blank space, you know that sooner or later someone will try to fill it.

'Outdoor' is a passive form of advertising that allows people to look if they are interested. It doesn't jump on you when you get in the door or appear unannounced in your inbox. This means it doesn't have any of the 'spam' feel associated with other, more direct forms of advertising.

Another plus is its flexibility – giving gardeners, for example, the option to advertise on tended roundabout flower beds or on park benches. It's local, flexible and in many cases gives your brand a lot of room to breathe.

But this laid-back approach has drawbacks – it is one of the easiest forms of advertising to ignore. It's possible to drive past a roadside board and, even if you're interested in the ad, miss the main message or the contact details.

Outdoor advertising is often run by specialist media agencies on behalf of local councils. Profits from the fees you pay will be split between the agency and the local authority. You can put your logo on just about anything from construction hoardings to lamppost banners, so just search for your target area and look up the solutions they offer.

Prices will vary depending on where you want to advertise, the size of your ad, how many people will see it and competition for the placement with other advertisers.

# TV AND RADIO

TV and radio are the big guns of the offline advertising world and it's unlikely that your budget will stretch this far, at least at first. If it does, congratulations – you have built a substantial business.

Costs will include:

- money spent on production
- studio hire
- the creative process (usually a 'story' dreamed up by a specialist agency)
- actors and voice actors (more for celebs)
- airtime.

Needless to say, it gets expensive. To give you a rough indication, the airtime alone for a week-long campaign on local radio could set you back £500 – that's before all other costs are factored in. For a regional station the same service could be £2,500 and a national might be £10,000-plus.

There is a potentially cheaper way to get on the TV or radio, however, and it's called PR.

> "Irrespective of your uniform or what van you drive, the first and most important thing in business is the quality of your work and your service. You can have all the tinsel, be on time and tidy up after yourself, but it counts for nothing if you do a bad job and the customer isn't happy.
>
> "You can break that down to relate to whatever business you are in. For us it starts with the call centre, the plumber does the job and then we do a follow-up to ensure everything went well and they're happy. From start to finish, this is the most important thing."
>
> – *Charlie Mullins, Pimlico Plumbers*

# PR

Public relations, also known as PR, aims to get you a lot of positive coverage in the media at a price point below that of running a widespread advertising campaign. The media – TV, radio, newspapers, magazines and online resources – are all looking for good stories that their audiences will want to read. PR is the act of developing these stories and feeding them to media sources to create exposure for clients.

The idea is that by being seen on TV, radio or in newspapers, you will become well-known and recognisable, even trusted, in your market. Businesses can use this exposure to develop new business and make additional sales.

PR takes many forms. You could set yourself up as a spokesperson for your industry, commenting in the local press on issues that impact businesses like yours. You could do something imaginative or even outlandish to attract attention – that might mean a hedge-pruning stunt, record-breaking Christmas lights or building an unusual garden room for a customer.

An agency will come up with a range of creative ideas much better than mine to put your business in the spotlight. They might suggest conducting a survey and publishing the results in a press release; the theme could be serious or funny and you would be the quoted spokesperson providing commentary or a quote to beef up the findings.

Like almost everything in this section, when it comes to PR you can spend as much or as little as you feel necessary. It's quite possible to get into the press without spending a penny (celebrities, MPs and sportspeople do it all the time).

But to ensure a methodical approach to public relations and to speed up your rise to fame, employing a PR agency will help enormously. Again, PR companies range from freelancers (cheap) to large-scale firms (expensive). A simple search online will reveal hundreds of options for you to investigate.

It's a good idea to approach a handful of firms to get an idea of cost and, importantly, what each business will do for their fees. Some charge a retainer, plus extras for specific work like a press release or a stunt. Work out your budget, stick to it and be clear about what you expect in return.

# WORD OF MOUTH

Research suggests that people are more likely to act on word-of-mouth recommendations than any advert or media coverage a company can muster. People trust their peers, or the majority view of the crowd, more than anything else – so it's important to encourage happy customers to spread the word about your good work.

Apart from being a compelling method for attracting new customers, the best thing about recommendations is that you don't need a marketing budget to get them. Just do a good job and ask that people remember you when asked to recommend a first-class plumber, electrician, landscape gardener etc.

It's amazing how quickly reputations can spread via workplaces, clubs, groups or parents at the school gate. You should never underestimate the power of recommendations. Leaving business cards or leaflets with happy customers might help prompt them to tell their friends.

Equally, word of mouth can work against you. So it's a good idea to ensure customers are happy. If you offer to put right anything they don't like – within reason – then you can avoid dents to your reputation.

Word-of-mouth recommendations come into their own online. The internet lets people communicate much faster than they can in the real world, so in the next chapter we'll cover the various ways you can take advantage of the fast-paced technological revolution happening all around us.

> "A lot of our lead generation comes from door-to-door canvassers and referrals from happy customers. We use the excellent Checkatrade and other accreditations for maximum benefits. We are certified by Certass, the CPA, FCA, Furniture Ombudsman, and Supalite."

**– Alan Gough, Warmglow Home Improvements Ltd**

# CHAPTER THREE

*Marketing Online*

# "It's so cheap and easy to market your business online, it would be criminal not to take advantage."

t's cheap and easy to market your business online, so much so that it would be criminal not to take advantage. In the sections below, you can read some of the main ways in which you can build a brand via the web.

> "We use Checkatrade which works well, and also appear near the top of Google. I think it is important to have a good professional website, with a professional picture and company logo. We have found that we also get recommendations through social media, as people will put a post looking for a decorator. LinkedIn is a good platform, as many other professionals have a profile on there."
>
> – **Chris Jones, LSW Decorating Ltd**

# WEBSITE

Your website performs a few key functions. It is your 'shop window', a contact centre, brand vehicle and communication medium. A good website should let you do the following:

- explain what you do and how you're better than the rest
- provide contact information so people can get in touch easily
- accept bookings instantly and without hassle
- receive feedback and respond to it
- post pictures and videos of work completed
- give an idea of your approach and what customers can expect
- publish testimonials from happy customers
- provide links to social media resources
- host DIY tips for small jobs
- write a blog about your profession
- list your pricing formula for different jobs.

The above list is pretty extensive and not everyone wants to spend lots of time online when they could be out building, fixing, tending and in general earning. But it shows you the scope of what's possible.

Let's start with the basics: it's very easy to set up a simple one-page website with all the essential information about your business. (In fact, your Checkatrade profile can also act as your website – saving time and effort.) If you don't have a website yet, you're not alone. Thousands of sole traders and small businesses haven't created one. But now is the time to change all that.

There are literally hundreds of services available to help you, some of which will cost you nothing more than a few hours of your time. You'll need basic computing skills, but no coding knowledge is required, and if you're a major technophobe then you can seek help from a family member or friend.

Type 'website builder UK' into a search engine and you'll find all the options: Wix, Squarespace, GoDaddy, 1&1, Fasthosts, Pickaweb – the list goes on and on. These range in prices and most offer a free service for a stripped-down product.

If you don't have an existing website, you'll need to pick a domain name. A domain is the word or words people write into an address bar to visit a website. Your domain should describe your business as closely as possible in a short phrase – but you might have to get creative as all of the most obvious phrases may already be taken.

If you have a brand name, use that. If the name is taken, try adding a word that describes your service – e.g. **www.cutanddryroofing.com** (which is available at the time of writing!). Adding this 'describing word' into your domain will help search engines and people understand your business quickly and easily.

Usually, the company that you buy a domain from (for about £8 a year) will host your website too. This just means it will provide the necessary connections and bandwidth to keep your website live and viewable.

The third part of the puzzle is the website itself. The companies listed above – and many others besides – give you the chance to create a personalised website using a simple system of selecting designs, picking detail elements and 'dragging and dropping' text, images and video.

The many design options on offer, together with your own logo and brand, guarantee a unique website unlike any of your competitors. Once you have the basic template you should add the essential information:

- business name and company number
- your logo
- a short description of your service, perhaps breaking this down into jobs your team can handle
- address and contact details
- pictures of you, your team, a job or anything else that adds colour to the page.

Should you wish to, you could give would-be customers more content. The more information you offer the happier they will be to pick up the phone. Consider any or all of the following:

- a blog about your jobs (where were they, what was needed and what you did)
- pictures and videos to illustrate your case studies
- a contact form, so that customers can see when you are available and even book jobs

- a feedback form so people can post reviews of your work
- links to social media pages like Facebook, Twitter and LinkedIn
- a price list for common jobs.

Many tradespeople have extended their reach by either writing (or, even better, videoing) simple tips, tricks and guides on how to complete small tasks without the help of professionals. At the end of the video they usually sign off with something like: *"If the problem is more complicated than this, you should call the experts on..."*.

Videos like these posted on YouTube (as well as the tradesperson's own website) often receive tens or even hundreds of thousands of views. A search for 'flat roof repair' on YouTube brings up a series of relevant videos with up to 500,000 views – a decent return on the time it takes to make the film!

If you already have an existing website but want to improve it, the process is essentially the same. Having created a site you're proud of, tell the host to dump the old site and make the new one live. They will take care of this and the switchover shouldn't take more than a day.

Websites are like anything in business – you tend to get out about as much as you put in. Make an effort with yours and you'll likely see it come back in the form of better marketing, more sales and an enhanced reputation.

But don't forget that you can start small and build it up as you get into the rhythm of online marketing!

# DIGITAL MARKETING AND SEO

Real-world marketing evolves quickly, with consumer tastes and new formats, but digital marketing changes at light speed. Marketing online is a science as much as an art, yet the equations that constitute 'getting it right' seem to move every year.

This is mainly because Google, the most popular search engine for English-speaking countries, is constantly tweaking and updating its algorithms to make searching better and more relevant to web users.

SEO, or search engine optimisation, is the act of making your website visible to Google and pushing it up to page one of search results by doing the sorts of things Google likes. It gets very complicated, but happily there are some fundamental rules about online marketing that don't change – and they're covered below.

## On-page SEO

'On-page SEO' refers to the basic structure and content of your website. It basically means building a good site, putting content in the right places and keeping it up-to-date and busy. Google prioritises web pages it sees as authoritative, safe and accessible, and it has a few methods to discover which websites are better than others.

If you create a website through a recognised website builder such as those listed above, then you can be sure the building blocks of your site are in the right place. It should pass all Google's basic tests. For example, it will be readable on all common devices like desktop computers, tablets (iPads and Kindles) and smartphones.

The next most important aspect of a popular website is its content. Google likes a lot of content and it prefers articles that are rich and thorough. As a general rule, it prefers longer articles over shorter ones and it likes pictures and video.

When it assesses your site – a process that happens automatically – it will weigh up what's there: are there lots of pages, is the content thorough and varied, is it being shared and talked about online, and do people value what they have seen? To get higher up in search engine rankings your website will have to answer all of these questions with a big 'yes'.

A straightforward one-page site has many important uses, but it won't appear in all but the most specific searches. Type a brief phrase that describes your area of expertise into Google – say 'electrician', 'painter and decorator' or 'kitchen fitter' – and you'll discover lots of big sites that are updated every day.

So, bigger is better when it comes to SEO, but other factors will help too. Google knows the location of many of its users, which means it's important to state clearly the area you operate in. If someone in Manchester searches for a plumber, it will often prioritise local businesses over ones further away.

Here's a nice introductory paragraph from Checkatrade member Heron Carpentry in Bromley, which helped take it to page one of Google in a local search for 'carpenter':

> *"Welcome To Heron Carpentry*
>
> *With 16 years' bespoke carpentry experience in Bromley, we specialise in kitchen fitting, new windows, window refurbishments, wooden and tiled flooring, garden decking and garden structures, built-in units, shelves, property restoration/maintenance, and first and second fix carpentry.*
>
> *Our qualified carpenters specialise in bespoke kitchens and all carpentry work in Bromley and London...*
>
> *Skill, creativity, honesty and reliability are all qualities that make a good carpenter. Once your project is completed, I am confident that you'll want to use Heron Carpentry's services again.*
>
> *Speak to one of our bespoke carpenters in Bromley for more information."*

There are seven references to *carpenter* or *carpentry*, leaving search engines in no doubt as to the business's area of operations. There are also references to 'experience', 'qualified', 'honesty' and 'reliability', which help visitors to the site understand its priorities.

There are also testimonials, examples of completed work and clear contact information. All this makes for a website that search engines will be comfortable pointing customers to.

## Off-page SEO

'Off-page SEO' refers to work beyond your website which brings relevant users to you. It can refer to social media posts, guest blogging, reaching out to online influencers and link building, to name a few standard techniques.

This type of marketing can be time-consuming, but it will give your business an edge online because of the simple fact that not many small businesses do it. It might seem strange to work on content for other people's websites instead of your own, but it's a proven method of business-building.

Essentially, the name of the game is to get your name out there and to spread your message across the internet. Writing articles for other websites is currently the most popular way to do this.

Let's say you're a gardener. The first thing to do is compile a list of gardening websites that are either popular or local or both. A web search for 'gardening magazine' throws up a few targets – for starters:

- **www.theenglishgarden.co.uk**
- **www.amateurgardening.co.uk**
- **www.moderngardensmagazine.co.uk**
- **www.thespruce.com**
- **www.gardensillustrated.com**
- **www.gardennewsmagazine.co.uk**

Add to this list the gardening sections of national newspapers, house and home titles and local news and information websites and you'll have a large hitlist in no time. Next think of five or six things you could write about – for example, lawn care, hedges, flower beds and pest control.

Next find the contact details for the editorial team and write a polite letter saying you want to write a really useful guide that you think readers will enjoy. Write a brief summary including information about what readers will learn.

Make sure to add that you're not expecting payment – editorial budgets are tight and website writers are always on the lookout for useful content that doesn't come with a fee! Then send the message and await responses.

Not everyone will respond, but if you have contacted a large number of websites with an enticing offer you should receive some emails back. If not, politely follow up with a reminder. The individual editors will have their own guidelines for written articles, including length and style, but they will give you a steer on this.

Next, write your column, making sure the language is up to scratch and free of spelling mistakes or grammatical errors – it's a good idea to get someone else to check this – and include your business name and a link to your website.

The value of this is threefold: first you get the immediate traffic to your website from readers interested to know more. Secondly, there will be an SEO effect – the link to your website tells Google it's worth reading (and this effect is magnified if people share the article around and link to it). Third, you can point to the piece in your own marketing materials – being published in a recognised journal is a big tick for your business.

A quicker route, which doesn't have quite the same bang but could nevertheless create a legion of new fans, is link building via forums and comment sections. Search for 'gardening forum' and read the conversations people are having online. If you can help, create an account, ideally placing a link in your user bio, and get chatting.

There are lots of opportunities to use words of wisdom online and people always appreciate good advice. The key is not to sell or advertise in these spaces, as doing so will get you labelled a 'spammer' and you'll more than likely be blacklisted. But carefully and considerately building a following by genuinely helping people will do the same job without angering forum users and commenters.

There are dozens of places to lend your gardening advice online and the same applies to electrical work, plumbing, roofing, carpentry, DIY and all areas of work. The best advice is to pick a small but relevant handful of these and do a little every day.

But if writing isn't your bag, then you could try making friends with people who already have popular blogs or video channels online. This is called 'outreach' and it basically means piggybacking on someone else's popularity.

A straightforward way to catch someone's eye is to offer a competition prize or free consultancy in return for some exposure and a link. You could try and secure a guest spot on a YouTube channel or a live Q&A session on a forum.

Again, it's essential to offer useful information or a sought-after prize that readers or viewers will really value. The website owner will appreciate the boost this will give their users and they might even welcome you back for a regular slot.

## Social media

Social media is another good example of off-page SEO. Having a busy Twitter, Facebook or Instagram account (among many other platforms) not only provides excellent Google-juice, it's also a great way to amass a dedicated following that you can convert into paying customers.

Social media is a very direct form of marketing, allowing you to connect directly with web users and supply them with simple crafted messages, including information about your business, sales, offers and competitions, words of inspiration, jobs completed and new staff being taken on.

All this creates a sense of community around your business and a story that's hard to replicate with other forms of marketing. People fear the unknown and the more you can do to break down this barrier by showing people your human side, the easier they will find it to get in touch and book your services. It's also a two-way channel of communication, so you can answer – or even ask – questions and receive feedback good, bad and indifferent.

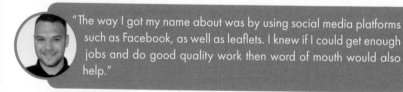

"The way I got my name about was by using social media platforms such as Facebook, as well as leaflets. I knew if I could get enough jobs and do good quality work then word of mouth would also help."

**– Matt Merry, Matt Merry Roofing**

# SUCCESS STORIES |||||➡

**Name:** Matt Merry
**Business name:** Matt Merry Roofing
**Type of business:** Roofing contractor
**Employees:** 2

### How did you get started in your trade?

"I got started in roofing after I finished a sports course at college. I hadn't enjoyed it and wanted something different. I was offered a job doing roofing – with the opportunity to learn the trade while working – so I took it."

### Has the business changed since you started?

"The business has changed a lot: for example, older and more traditional methods which I learned when I started roofing have now been replaced by newer methods and systems that last longer."

### Describe your typical customer and project.

"My typical customers are homeowners close to the area I live (Hinckley). Typical projects range from small repair jobs to full re-roofs and I also do a little bit of industrial roofing work."

### What do you enjoy about your career?

"I enjoy working outside in the fresh air, getting some great views of the local area and meeting new people every day."

### What's the hardest thing about it, or the biggest challenge you face?

"Now that I'm set up and established in the local area there isn't anything too hard, but to start with the hardest part was getting regular and constant work."

### What are your plans for the future?

"My plans for the future are to continue with what I'm doing now, and then to learn new aspects of roofing to add to the list of services I provide my customers. I also want to expand the area I cover."

### What's your best tip for other tradespeople in your sector?

"When you start, make sure you have money behind you to deal with quiet patches that will more than likely come. Do your best to make strong and lasting working relationships with customers, they'll help to bring in more work through word of mouth."

If you are stuck over where to begin, check out some popular pages on your favourite social media sites. DIY is a popular general topic, so simply type into a search engine 'DIY Instagram' or 'DIY Twitter' for instant inspiration.

Each social media platform has its own identity and a different group of followers, so it's important to recognise that what works for one might not work for another. They also work in subtly different ways. For example, Instagram is for quick flicks through pictures, while Facebook allows for long complicated posts that can take several minutes to read.

It's a good idea to read up on your target media and make sure it works for you. Snapchat has a young audience compared to Twitter, so you might want to target the latter in preference to the former, for example.

# EMAIL

One of the oldest methods of online marketing is email marketing, yet when done right it is still arguably the most effective. For one thing, it is a dominant means of communication. It is estimated that, globally, around 3.7bn people have an email address – that's 1.5bn more than have a Facebook account.

Email is also a captive audience: if you send an email then someone will receive it – the same can't be said for a social media post or a blog on a website. It also targets users where they work, because millions of us read email every day as part of our jobs.

But email comes with a couple of downsides. For a start you have to create a database of addresses, which is becoming increasingly difficult as governments clamp down on data protection. You also have to justify sending an email by creating good content that people really want to read.

But these issues notwithstanding, this medium can be a real winner. Even a small database of 100 or so addresses can yield a healthy return of sales if treated with respect and kept up to date.

To create a list you have to ask each individual's permission. This can be done via a newsletter sign-up on your website or in person as you meet people and complete jobs for them. It takes time to build something that will attract a lot of business, but the effort is usually worth it.

When you have some email addresses and some content to send them, search for a reputable email marketing platform. These include MailChimp, Mailjet, SendGrid, Campaign Monitor and Constant Contact. All offer a free solution for small lists of emails and low rates of sending each month.

They try to make it easy for you to upload your list of email addresses and to create attractive newsletters for your readers with the minimum of fuss. Once you have created a template, you can use it again and again by filling it with fresh content each time you do a mail out.

A word of warning, however: email can feel intrusive and it doesn't take a lot to make email users angry if they are targeted without their permission or even if they do give permission but receive too many emails. Keep your messages sparing and useful for the best results!

# GETTING REGISTERED ON CHECKATRADE

Checkatrade membership provides you with the tools to not only increase your exposure among the millions of consumers using its website every year but to also build your physical reputation through online feedback.

Why join? Here are just a few reasons:

- It doesn't sell leads – receive calls from genuine customers with no competitive bidding for work.
- A comprehensive web profile for your business.
- Monthly payment option with no upfront charge or checking fee.
- Access to over 1.3m website visits every month.
- Dedicated membership advice team to offer support throughout your membership.
- Exclusive offers and discounts from leading brands, allowing you to save more than the cost of your membership.
- The sign of quality which affiliation with **Checkatrade.com** provides.
- Members' Area allowing you to manage your profile and monitor the performance of your membership.
- You can also choose to be included in one of its printed directories. Deployed to around 50,000 homes in your local area, these are an effective tool for maximising the reach and exposure of your business – particularly amongst a non-digital audience.

"Having dwindling results from print-based advertising, we now rely on web-based marketing, using Checkatrade as our main (90%) source of work. The review system has been amazing at showing the type of work we do and the pride we take in that, leading to recommendation work off the back of jobs completed after initial Checkatrade leads."

**– Chris Fairbairn, Cribbit Installations Ltd**

"I've worked for my father since I left school at 17. Most of our work came from recommendations and word of mouth, but today a lot of people use the internet to gain access to trades and after joining Checkatrade I've never looked back."

**– Simon Baker, Simon Baker Plumbing & Heating Ltd**

Here are some of the ways in which Checkatrade is becoming even more useful.

## 1. Tripling its marketing spend to £15m

In 2017 Checkatrade spent around £5m on marketing to grow its trader network and drive consumer traffic to its website, generating more jobs for trades businesses like yours. In 2018 it planned to spend nearly £15m on those areas – increasing TV and radio coverage and online advertising on Google, Facebook and other media channels. This included highly localised activity. Checkatrade have tested it and found it extremely successful.

## 2. Over 5m additional local printed directories

Directories are Checkatrade's foundation. It's now making them better, reaching more customers in existing and new areas. It's got a new model that will increase coverage from 35% of UK homeowners and see it increase total distribution from 20m to over 25m. It is also testing new creative approaches and the frequency with which they are sent out, while looking into how to maximise the number of calls and web visits they generate for members.

## 3. New emergency jobs

Checkatrade Now is the new emergency service giving members more jobs. Emergency and small jobs represent millions of jobs per year and Checkatrade thinks this is a great opportunity for its members. Checkatrade Now is the solution for consumers who require emergency work and need to fix it very quickly. As a member you will be able to sign up to Checkatrade Now and when emergency jobs come up in your chosen area, if you are available, you'll be able to accept jobs through the Checkatrade Now app on your phone. Checkatrade is letting members know as this service comes to their area. Visit **Checkatrade.com/now** to register your interest.

## 4. Save money with the Checkatrade Buying Club

Checkatrade is using its buying power to create a new service, Checkatrade Buying Club, which will give you discounts and savings on the brands, services, parts, materials and tools you use the most such as fuel, equipment, PLI and vehicles – things that are critical to your business.

Checkatrade has a huge selection of goods at the very best prices exclusively for its members. New deals will be added regularly, starting with the launch of a brand new partnership established with a major parts and tools provider.

## 5. Software to make running your business easier

Checkatrade has developed its own software in conjunction with its sister company in Spain. The new software will be launched in late 2018 and will help with the following:

- managing your customer information
- managing your jobs to ensure you stay on top of your workload
- creating and sending quotes/invoices directly.

# 6. Visibility on the amount of business you are receiving and reducing nuisance calls

Just like its directories, Checkatrade is introducing optional managed numbers (and emails) to its website. This means that each member will have their own unique, traceable contact details. This improvement will allow Checkatrade to provide members with the following:

- You can see how many calls and emails have been generated from your Checkatrade profile, including how many calls you have missed.

- If members are being targeted en masse by nuisance calls, Checkatrade can block them at source, stopping all their calls to its members.

- Managed numbers will give peace of mind to consumers. If a member leaves, Checkatrade can redirect the call to a current checked and monitored member.

This has already been introduced in the Central West region and, in April alone, Checkatrade logged over 24,900 calls and 8,500 emails – an average of over 20 contacts per member per month in that region!

# 7. Improved members area

Through a new personalised dashboard, you will be able to access and review the performance of your membership through impressions on your profile page and work alerts. Checkatrade is also adding a powerful new monitoring and reporting tool.

As well as continuing to see how many times your company page has been chosen and clicked on by consumers and continuing to understand how many request callbacks have been generated, you will be able to see how many emails have been sent to you via Checkatrade and how many calls you have received.

*To become a part of the Checkatrade network, simply visit* **Checkatrade.com/join** *or call the team on 0345 2411 393.*

"My customers are encouraged to submit feedback to the Checkatrade website. This delivers an excellent platform for new customers to decide where to go and who to choose. Checkatrade has kept my company name out there and creates a continuous flow of enquiries."

**– Jane Pennock, Us Girls Decorating Ltd**

# CHAPTER FOUR

*Building Your Sales*

"A steady stream of loyal customers lessens the need to attract new ones, so you spend less time on marketing and fewer sleepless nights wondering where the next job will come from."

**G**enerating sales means more than just marketing and advertising. These two areas of business will put your business in front of a lot of potential customers, but there remains the significant job of completing the sale and laying the foundations for repeat custom in the months and years ahead.

A steady stream of loyal customers lessens the need to attract new ones, so you spend less time on marketing and fewer sleepless nights wondering where the next job will come from. It's good for reputation, increases the chances that people will recommend you and provides a solid, dependable platform from which your business can grow.

> "We have found that the key to sales is being proficient at customer contact, especially in the early stages. Get back to initial enquiries quickly to show you are keen and interested in the work, produce quality quotes that are clear and explain exactly what is being offered, what is included (don't leave anything out) and follow up, follow up, follow up!"

*– Chris Fairbairn, Cribbit Installations Ltd*

In this chapter, we'll examine what it takes to make ongoing sales, how you can approach selling in a methodical way and what you can do to ensure customers are left with the contented feeling of knowing they have paid a fair price for a job well done.

# SALES STRATEGY

It's possible – perhaps even probable – that you've never considered the idea of a sales strategy before. But as your business grows, creating one will ensure a coordinated approach that delivers the best results. Unless you agree sales goals and a route to hitting these targets, your approach risks becoming incoherent and patchy, potentially leading to lower revenue and missed opportunities.

A strategy will help you understand your market and will make decisions – such as where to spend on advertising, which jobs to accept and reject and who to hire – a whole lot clearer. Many sole traders wait for calls and decide on the spot whether they will take a job or decline it, which is fine, but isn't sustainable for a business with real potential.

To earn that potential you need to come up with some ideas as to how you'll move forward. A sales strategy should cover:

- **Clear priorities** – where is the low-hanging fruit and how can you grab it?
- **Simple outcomes** – what should happen if you do what you say you will?
- **Guidelines** – how should people act to get where you want to go?
- **Goals** – after doing all the above, where should you be in a year's, or three years', time?

The act of thinking these elements through and writing them down should help you make decisions that will benefit your business in the long term, while driving down the potential for wasted effort or wrong turns.

Your sales strategy is the opportunity to approach business coherently instead of making decisions based on temporary or immediate factors that don't take into account the big picture. It's a bit like the difference between planning a holiday and just jumping in the car with no flights or accommodation booked – and without packing a suitcase.

Breaking down the contents of your sales strategy, you should consider coming up with your ideal contract (being realistic). These are the kind of jobs that will take you to the next level. Think of the factors that will make this transition a reality, by working out the strengths, weaknesses, opportunities and threats that make it more or less likely to happen.

A SWOT analysis, as this is labelled, is a standard method of planning used by big businesses of all descriptions. For a multinational corporation, the opportunities and threats are on a global scale – for you they might be more local, but just as relevant to a positive outcome.

First, review the last 12 months and assess what went right, what went wrong and what could have been done to improve what happened. Even if you had a good year, this exercise will give you some insight as to areas of the business that could be fine-tuned.

For example, you could ask:

- How much revenue did you make?
- From how many contracts?
- If you have a team, who was the strongest performer and why?
- What was your best and worst feedback (pick a few examples)?
- What was your best job in terms of benefit to your business?
- Did you improve on the year before – if so, what made the difference?
- Are you in a better or worse place than you were 12 months ago?

Now, think about the next 12 months: are there big events that you can benefit from? Perhaps a new shopping centre is about to be commissioned or a local park is due a revamp. Could you get in early with a pitch? For threats, think of local spending power, your competition, your own competences and staffing – what could get in the way?

You'll start to paint a picture illustrating a clear plan of attack as well as the actions you must take to accentuate the positives and dilute the risks.

Next, think of your sales target. If your revenue is, say, £200,000 a year, what must happen in order for that to grow to £300,000? Your

SWOT analysis coupled with your revenue target will combine to create an action plan, which is where to begin your pursuit of business growth.

Remember the old adage that in business 80% of revenue comes from 20% of customers? It's not as relevant to a small trades business as a large media agency, for example, but it is right in pointing out that some customers will be a lot more valuable than others.

If you already have a team, even if it's just one person, include them in this process. You could start from scratch and work on it as a team, or you could draw up a skeleton plan and ask your people to lend their feedback and ideas to the mix.

If your team is involved in the process they are much more likely to understand the process and your goals, plus (and this is important) they will be more motivated to assist you in making it all happen.

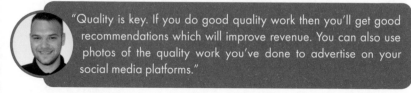

"Quality is key. If you do good quality work then you'll get good recommendations which will improve revenue. You can also use photos of the quality work you've done to advertise on your social media platforms."

*– Matt Merry, Matt Merry Roofing*

# PITCHING AND QUOTING

So, you've assessed your market position, considered improvements to your business and prepared for an upswing in sales. You've upgraded your marketing and advertising so that a stream of future customers know about your brand. Next is the thorny issue of pitching for work, agreeing a price and – ideally – improving your payday with some optional extra services.

Pitching is both a science and an art. You have to make a customer excited (ideally) in your vision for them, but also comfortable with the price you want to charge. The difficulty of getting this balance right is plain to see – even some of the biggest government contractors with billions of pounds of revenue occasionally get into hot water because they price too low or overpromise and underdeliver.

Go in too low – perhaps for a high-profile contract – and you risk eating into profit margins or, worse, making a loss. But pitch too high and you might be met with raised eyebrows and a polite 'thanks but no thanks'.

This is a tightrope walk, admittedly, and it's very important to factor in all costs. Many of these are obvious, such as parts and labour for the duration of the contract. Others less so, such as wear and tear on equipment (depreciation), fuel and delays, which all must be factored in.

As a customer, it's always a nasty shock to be presented with an extra bill, regardless whether it is calculated in an itemised list of expenses, so make sure you and your customer understands all costs *before* you get started.

> "Generally, we have a daily rate and I work out how many days a job will take and quote from there. We have thought about having a price-matching policy, but I am also conscious of the need to meet wages. Sometimes on a larger job we will give sections out on a price."

**– Chris Jones, LSW Decorating Ltd**

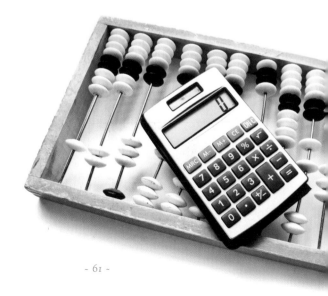

# SUCCESS STORIES ||||▌▶

**Name:** Chris Jones
**Business name:** LSW Decorating
**Type of business:** Decorating and property renovation
**Number of employees:** 3

### How did you get started in your trade?

"When I left school, I attended college and completed an apprenticeship. From there, I have been involved in decorating and property renovation for over 15 years."

### Has the business changed since you started?

"Since starting the business, the main change has been to quickly adapt to enter into the commercial market. We achieved this by becoming VAT-registered, which is more attractive for businesses. We have also branched out to offer other small works such as carpentry. We priced for various trades and drew up different contacts."

### Describe your typical customer and project.

"Our typical customers tend to be private homeowners or companies."

### What do you enjoy about your career?

"The thing that I enjoy the most is picking up lots of tips for renovating a property at a reduced cost. For example, recently I was working in a home where a customer had a nice bowl from China as a sink. She mentioned she had a glasscutter create the waste-pipe hole. There are a lot of tips and tricks of this nature that I have picked up over the years.

Living in London, I also enjoy meeting a range of different customers."

### What's the hardest thing about it, or the biggest challenge you face?

"The hardest thing has probably been running every aspect of the business, such as accounts, IT, quoting, invoicing, and managing projects. I needed to adapt and take certain days off during the month to focus on HMRC submissions. I also have the option to outsource some admin work if needed."

### What are your plans for the future?

"Our plan is to adapt and grow as a company. We plan to become a small construction company involved in purchasing property for renovation."

### What's your best tip for other tradespeople in your sector?

"I would recommend becoming a limited company, as opposed to being a sole trader. I would also recommend diversifying to branch out into other areas within the industry."

When pitching for bigger jobs its important to keep in mind the fundamental principles of profit and loss. Sometimes it's better to refuse a job than to take it on under the wrong terms, especially if it means missing out on another one that's more appropriate.

Your sales strategy gives you a good idea of the jobs that will really boost your business; it's worth making extra effort for these, but not at any cost.

Let's assume there's a juicy contract in the offing, one that will represent a good chunk of your projected annual revenue and that will allow you to invest in further growth. The terms are right and the work is within your scope.

It's likely you'll be up against some stiff competition, so your pitch had better be good. Most customers look for value first and foremost, but many can be persuaded by a grand vision. 'Painting a picture' or 'telling a story' might sound a bit overbaked, particularly if the pitch is for something functional like new locks, a drainage system or insulation, but consider the following: none of the most successful companies sell the nuts and bolts of what they do.

Nike doesn't sell trainers, Apple doesn't sell tech and Airbnb doesn't sell accommodation. They all sell a lifestyle, freedom, fun and experiences.

Big sports brands are all about achieving your fitness goals and emulating superstar athletes; the branding of major banks links what they do with your family, your comfort and your security; technology companies want you to become a better, more efficient person.

Take a leaf (however small) out of their books. You're not selling plumbing, insulation or locks – it's safety, security, convenience and peace of mind. Clients want to know that they can rely on your work and will continue to enjoy its benefits for years to come.

So sprinkle a little magic dust into the pitch to illustrate what they will get, above the physical service you can provide. A compelling pitch adds colour and flavour. It communicates everything that the customer needs to know, plus something extra to engage them.

## An important caveat

A common problem with pitches is that they focus on the service provider and not enough on the customer. Describing your abilities is essential, of course, but understanding the customer is equally so.

So do some research, find out the customer's pain-points and make sure you fully understand the parameters of the project, not just your bit of it but the whole thing. What are their priorities? Do they need something quick or will they value constant contact above all? Have they suffered problems in the past?

Make sure the pitch addresses all of the key concerns and include in it some words that show the customer you understand where they are coming from. You don't need to include their complete history, but do include some details that prove you've done your homework.

If you're pitching in person then it's a good idea to take along something visual for the customer to look at. This could be an on-screen presentation, but it could just as easily be handouts, or models or examples of past work.

Providing something tangible will break up the pitch and lengthen attention spans. Clients are more likely to remember pictures than words, too.

It almost goes without saying that pitches should be friendly but professional, informative but to-the-point and, if there is more than one person presenting, then everyone should have rehearsed their role in the pitch to ensure it is fluid and memorable for the right reasons.

After the pitch it might be worth following up with a polite email, thanking the team for hearing your pitch and hoping they found it valuable. It will help to reinforce their memory of you and underline your keenness to do the work.

# UPSELLING

If you win the pitch, there is an opportunity to beef up the job by offering value-added services not included in the original brief. This requires delicacy. In many cases, upselling won't be appropriate because customers are looking for solutions to specific problems. But if you can see room for additional services, and have struck up a good rapport with the customer, then give it go.

Here are a few areas in which you can upsell:

- higher quality products and materials that give better profit margin
- an extended service with ongoing support
- a new aspect to the job, or extra work not mentioned in the pitch
- work on other projects being carried out by the same customer.

If you identify an area in which you can offer something extra, then start a conversation. This approach should be less formal than your original pitch and should start along the lines of: *"We noticed X aspect of the project, did you ever consider doing Y? We could offer you Z."*

It should be framed as an optional upgrade and in no way should it sound like a deal-breaker. If you're unsure how a second approach will be received, it's best to make do with the deal you have worked so hard to win.

It's possible your new customer will want to negotiate terms at this point too, with a view to reducing the price. In this case you need to be firm – don't be tempted to cut your fee unless you can also save money by reducing the scope of the job.

Remember that profit margins and reputation are at stake on every project and that sometimes it's better to walk away than to risk losing money or hard-earned status.

"Sometimes a customer will do the upselling for you. If they are happy with the work but want something to change then be prepared to accommodate them. You'll be paid again so there is no reason to complain.

"I tend to schedule in jobs with a measure of flexibility, which allows me to run over on a job if the customer wants to add something or change what they originally ask for. I wouldn't recommend stacking up jobs because they so often run over for one reason or another. Remember to love the customer you're with!"

*– Wayne de Wet, Wayne de Wet Painting and Decorating Services*

# CUSTOMER SERVICE

In business there are two key areas from a customer's point of view: the product or service you provide and the way in which you provide it. The second is often just as important as the first. For online retailers, for example, customer service means easy and quick delivery, ready communication, a simple returns policy and engaging brand messaging.

For a tradesperson it's even more vital, because you're so often in contact with people in their homes and places of work. Many people are uncomfortable around strangers, especially young men, so going the extra mile to put them at ease will win you plaudits.

"We have got where we are today through hard work. No great mystery or lucky break, just hours and hours of input. Anybody with their own business will know there is no such thing as a 40-hour week! In the beginning the business literally consumed our lives, but seven years in, we have established some balance.

"The reputation we built for ourselves generates business for us on a daily basis. That reputation was built with kindness, dedication and respect. Even now, for every customer, for every job, I try to see things from their point of view. I answer questions before customers ask them, I note small things that will make customers' lives easier. We have maintained professionalism and integrity."

*– Louise Kirk, RH Heating and Plumbing Ltd*

Here's a quick list of other ways to deliver first-rate customer service:

# 1. Be kind, friendly and thoughtful

Manners go a long way in business and people appreciate others who are approachable. But not everyone has a good understanding of the best way to behave around customers. If you're worried, give your team a pep talk.

Pleases and thank-yous should come as standard, as should thoughtful extras such as asking if it's OK to wear your boots in the house, closing exterior doors where possible to keep heat in, and tidying up as much as is reasonable at the end of each day.

Much of this might sound obvious, but does everyone in your team understand how important good manners is – and how not observing them could cost the business?

# 2. Do the knowledge

Clients often have questions and they might not know who to ask. Make sure your team knows who they are working for, what the main goals of the project are, timescales, locations and any other information that might prove essential.

If someone is asked a question they can't answer, they should promise to find out and have a direct line to someone else in the know.

# 3. Listen and respond positively

Complex projects like building extensions, bathroom fittings, landscaping and large cleaning contracts don't always go to plan. This is a fact of life and no matter how much you plan, unforeseeable problems and delays can creep in.

If a delay occurs, tell the customer straight away, explain why the problem cropped up and suggest a way to fix it. This will satisfy many people, but sometimes – for whatever reason – a customer will have a gripe to air. Don't argue with them; listen, remain calm and take a moment to respond in a sympathetic way.

You don't have to admit you're in the wrong if you're not, but getting involved in a shouting match won't help you, the customer, the job or your reputation.

## 4. Go the extra mile

If it doesn't cost you anything, a five-minute job here and there outside the scope of your brief will boost your standing with your customer. Positive reviews online are full of stories about tradespeople who went out of their way to help.

## 5. Offer a warranty

You know your work is top quality, but if this is your first job with a customer then they can't be completely sure. Offering a warranty, for example to repair any fair-usage wear for 12 months, will give them added peace of mind.

## 6. Check back

A project doesn't finish when the last nail is hammered in. It's good practice to follow up after a week or so to ask if your customer is completely satisfied. Invite feedback and, if it's roundly positive, ask if they would be happy to write you a review on Checkatrade.

Circling back to happy customers will cement your reputation and increases the chances you'll be asked back when a new project is up for grabs. Also, people appreciate the gesture because it shows you care.

"Over the last five years my plumbing business has grown stronger and stronger. This is because I take sincere ownership of jobs and provide great service to my customers. Simple things like taking my shoes off in people's houses shows respect and gives potential customers confidence. It wins us lots of jobs.

"The Checkatrade feedback programme has been very influential on my business growth: in this day and age of social media frenzy, word of mouth on its own is not enough to really grow a business."

**– Godfrey Muneri, C&G Plumbers Ltd**

# SUCCESS STORIES ▐▐▐▐▶

**Name:** Godfrey Muneri
**Business name:** C&G Plumbers
**Type of business:** Plumbing
**Number of employees:** 4

### How did you get started in your trade?

"I was a franchisee owner for four years before, by chance, I watched a programme on TV about the amount of money tradespeople can earn. I got in touch with a plumbing institute, enrolled on a course and then trained to become a plumber."

### Has the business changed since you started?

"The first year was quite a challenge. I had to build a portfolio and a customer base, but since then business has grown year on year. In one year my turnover increased by more than 100% compared to the previous one."

### Describe your typical customer and project.

"They are usually domestic customers. Jobs include basic repair work, bathroom installations and emergency call-out."

### What do you enjoy about your career?

"The best thing about this job is delivering customer satisfaction and helping people."

### What's the hardest thing about it, or the biggest challenge you face?

"The hardest thing about the job is the fact that you can't please everyone."

### What are your plans for the future?

"Ideally I'd like to have more than three vans on the road working for customers in my area."

### What's your best tip for other tradespeople in your sector?

"It's true that the customer is always right. You should respect them and their homes."

# CHAPTER FIVE

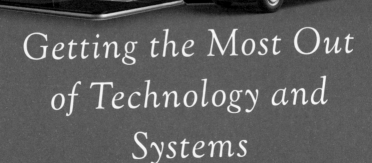

*Getting the Most Out of Technology and Systems*

"It's a fair bet that your most useful gadget is a smartphone, but these devices can do so much more than send messages and receive calls."

**A**ll businesses use technology in one way or another. Today, it's a fair bet that your most useful gadget is a smartphone, but these devices can do so much more than send messages and receive calls. They are the new personal organisers, capable of running complex systems and growing businesses.

New software and apps let you organise, communicate and prepare. There are apps for HR, payroll, invoicing and 'customer relationship management' or CRM. Adopting and mastering just a handful of these tools gives you power to organise your business, making it leaner, more efficient and potentially more profitable.

Any software worth its salt should allow you access from any device – password-protected, of course. It should let you share access, or bits of information, with other team members and the information you input should be updated in real-time, so that everyone is kept up to date with the changes you make.

"Last year we introduced a digital signing system. The overheads on this were quite large but it's much, much easier than getting people to sign and return documents. All employees can log on to the online system and see when a customer signed and what for without trying to track down the paperwork. We work across multiple locations and this has really reduced internal phone calls."

*– Adam Allsop, The Shutter Studio Ltd*

# SUCCESS STORIES |||||⟶

**Name:** Adam Allsop
**Business name:** The Shutter Studio
**Type of business:** Bespoke shutters and carpentry
**Number of employees:** 21

### How did you get started in your trade?

"I started working on building sites as a teenager and learnt the basics of everything, but woodworking was the only thing I really enjoyed. Everything followed naturally from there."

### Has the business changed since you started?

"Clients have a lot more information now compared to when we started. They've done their research online so it's important to know your products inside out."

### Describe your typical customer and project.

"A typical project will be for a proud homeowner who wants to spend some time making their space something that truly works for them and reflects them. We do a wide variety of styles and products, but the care taken for the customer is always the same."

### What do you enjoy about your career?

"I enjoy seeing ideas come to life. You can't underestimate the impact of seeing something you collaborated on and built, installed and ready to go."

**What's the hardest thing about it, or the biggest challenge you face?**

"It's bit of a cliche, but we're squeezed from all sides by taxes. Fuel duty is a major one, and business rates have gone up for all of our business locations."

**What are your plans for the future?**

"We've just started a sister organisation, The Carpentry Studio, so the next step is to build the brand and reputation to the same size as The Shutter Studio."

**What's your best tip for other tradespeople in your sector?**

"Always be thinking about how you can make life easier for you and the customer. Cutting small bits of friction where you can will get you huge savings in the long run."

Here are just a few business functions that can receive a real boost from technology:

# CUSTOMER RELATIONSHIP MANAGEMENT (CRM)

It costs a lot more time and effort to attract new customers than it does to retain existing ones, so 'managing' your customers is vital. Good CRM software should be accessible by a modern mobile phone and should cover important tasks such as:

* storing customer contact details
* handling all kinds of communication
* scheduling meetings, pitches and projects
* managing teams
* creating special offers and discounts.

There are a lot of products to choose from, many of which – including HubSpot, Salesforce, Bullhorn and Capsule – offer free trials, discounted offers for small businesses or are even entirely free to use. It's worth picking a few of these and trying them out before deciding which is your favourite. One thing's for sure, it beats writing everything down in a notepad!

> "In the first year, paperwork was overwhelming – from gas reports to invoicing, quotes and landlord reports. I downloaded a free app which lets me produce gas reports and invoices before I've even left a customer's property. I've used apps to register boilers and order my stock.
>
> "I used to carry a few different handheld devices, from distance-measuring tools to thermal imaging cameras. I invested in a CAT S60 mobile phone which brings most of these things into my mobile phone. It lets me produce professional reports to customers and even include thermal images of problems. This reassures them that what I'm saying is the truth and so far 100% of the customers I have produced reports for have given us the work."

**– Jordan Williams, JR Williams Plumbing Services Ltd**

> "Over the first year of the business I've developed a system of integrated online apps to automate and streamline many of the standard processes of the customer journey.
>
> "These processes extend to: management of the customers' information in a CRM; their stage in the deal pipeline and self-scheduling of surveys and installations, complete with automatic follow-up and reminders. It also helps to generates quotes and invoices and dispatch subcontractors.
>
> "This high level of automation, coupled with the near total elimination of any duplicate data entries, has made it possible to successfully coordinate so many installs within one year. In an industry not generally recognised for its high level of adoption of computer technology, this approach has given us an advantage."

**– Andrew Johnstone, Loft Boarding Scotland Ltd**

# HR

Many top business thinkers believe businesses should put their staff ahead of their customers. If workers are happy, the theory goes, then customers will benefit hugely from an engaged, enthusiastic and well-trained workforce.

Whether you agree with this principle or not, it's unarguable that managing your people – hiring and firing, payroll, holidays, sick leave, performance, benefits, training and team activities – is a vital part of a well-oiled machine.

Luckily, there is a huge array of software that can do the job clearly and easily, with intuitive designs and simple ways to input new data. Products like breatheHR, SMB, Cascade HR and Youmanage have been created to store reams of information in simple formats.

They are low-cost, often based on a subscription model, and flexible, giving you the option to scale up staff numbers as the business develops. It beats working through a cluttered spreadsheet. Run a search online for a huge list of options.

> "Other than the normal computer software to communicate, produce estimates and invoices, I use a basic PAYE tool to keep connected with HMRC. Once you know how to use this, it gives you peace of mind and keeps you on track with payments. The overriding piece of technology for me is Checkatrade – it serves as advertising and reporting, plus it really does 'pat you on the back'."

**– Jane Pennock, Us Girls Decorating Ltd**

# FINANCE

Finance covers a range of money-related issues, from accounting and invoicing, to securing a loan and winning investment to grow your business. In chapter 7, we'll look at this in more detail – in this tech-focused chapter we'll just cover the growing suite of apps that put you in full control of your finances.

It's often said that cash flow is king. Plenty of good, viable businesses go to the wall every year because invoices were paid late or too much money went out before payments came in, so keeping a close eye on your cash is key to building a sustainable business.

As with CRM and HR there's a good choice of finance apps (over and above what your bank can supply), so it's worth shopping around and finding the best fit.

## Invoicing and accounting

Big platforms in invoicing and accounting include market leaders like Xero and QuickBooks, as well as newer offerings such as Wave and KPMG's small business software. Prices and functionality vary, but the base level is a full picture of your venture's financial health.

That means the ability to create, send and track invoices, view cash flow information, log expenses, track vehicle mileage, run a tax self-assessment, track and pay VAT and run your payroll – all from a desktop computer, tablet or smartphone.

"We spent a lot of time and money developing our own CRM system. This helps the business massively, as every single customer is guided through a smooth process for whatever job they are having done. The CRM makes it easy for our install department to manage multiple jobs and make sure all payments due are collected on time and efficiently.

"We also manage a separate diary for salespeople, fitters, surveys and lead management. It's a huge asset to our business and will allow us to continue our rapid growth."

*– Alan Gough, Warmglow Home Improvements Ltd*

## Expenses

Claiming expenses can be a tricky affair for staff. Often they have to buy materials or pay for transport out of their own pockets before billing their employer later on (with fingers crossed that the boss will agree it's a viable spend).

But there are apps available to do this process automatically, before someone has to dip into their own cash. Concur is a good example of such software; it lets users book work trips and submit expense claims to be approved by a manager.

For businesses that do a lot of travelling, the app can be used to negotiate preferable rates for trips, particularly airfares. One for bigger businesses, perhaps, but worth keeping in mind for discounts down the line.

"We use Sage One to run the business accounts. We can run the payroll, as well as all invoicing and bookkeeping. We have also considered using a card payment service at some point, which is also available through Sage One.

"We also use Moneypenny, as a PA call-answering service. This is important, because some customers may not always leave a voicemail. We also have a landline directed to my mobile phone. This also looks more professional for online advertising, as opposed to a mobile number."

**– Chris Jones, LSW Decorating Ltd**

## Closing investments

If you have real ambition for your business, you might consider raising an equity investment, meaning convincing a person or fund to invest in your business in return for a stake in your venture. Not many private equity or venture capital houses feature an app, but increasingly crowdfunding companies do.

Crowdfunding companies put you in touch with large groups of private investors who can plough in money from £10 to the total amount you require. Organisations like Crowdcube, Seedrs and Crowdfunder all offer either apps or mobile-friendly websites, so you can track investments in real time on the go. For more on raising money, check out chapter 9.

As well as apps that are great for general purposes, there is of course a wealth of technology – hardware and software – that helps tradespeople do their job faster, more efficiently and to a higher standard. The list is too long and varied to go into here; suffice to say that it's always worth keeping an eye out for digital tools of the trade that can boost your business.

> "Investing in 3D rendering software to produce photo-quality renders of what completed projects will look like has been an excellent move for us, almost replacing the need for a showroom. We stock samples of tiles, flooring and doors so customers can see and feel the real thing in their own home.
>
> "We have also invested in a quote system that allows us to easily and quickly produce quality, clear and branded quotes."

*– Chris Fairbairn, Cribbit Installations Ltd*

# VEHICLES AND EQUIPMENT

They say a tradesperson is only as good as their tools. This is half right, in that good equipment leads to an easier job, a better finish and impressed customers. As mentioned in the 'branding' section (chapter 2), first impressions count and people will want reassurances that you're up to the job.

A muddy, unbranded van with a messy driver's cabin is the worst possible start, as is the sight of a tradesperson struggling over tasks with old or otherwise inadequate kit. Think of new tools as more of an investment than an expense. They will pay you back many times over their lifetime.

"A good van with a bright, attractive design is important for a brand, as well as also being free advertising and looking professional."

**– Chris Jones, LSW Decorating Ltd**

Make sure you get adequate insurance and, if possible, lock up your equipment in a secure place (not your vehicle) overnight to avoid falling victim to opportunistic thieves. If you have to leave tools in your van, be prepared with good locks and a modern alarm – better safe than sorry, as they say.

Let's start with your transportation. Commercial vehicles are a big area of business for major manufacturers, which means there is a lot of competition in the market. Top brands include Fiat, Volkswagen, Ford and Vauxhall, with many more besides.

Key considerations for purchasing a vehicle include manufacturer reputation, fuel consumption, ruggedness and cubic space. It's a good idea to ask a few questions before you sign on the dotted line:

- How much space do you need?
- Are most of your jobs local, regional or national?
- How much does it cost to tax and insure the vehicle?
- Will it be easy to customise and brand?
- Are there any other special requirements unique to your business?

When making your decision, remember to factor in large jobs which might require a little more of everything. You don't want to have to pass on a project because you can't move items from A to B, although hiring additional capacity is an option in such cases too.

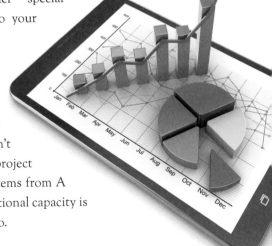

When you know what you want, next comes the thorny issue of paying for your new vehicle. A large transit van could set you back £20,000 + VAT, while a smaller 'courier' size vehicle can start anywhere from £10,000 + VAT.

This is clearly a major outlay, especially if you're building a fleet for a growing business, but luckily there are numerous ways to pay other than settling the full price upfront. All vehicle finance packages essentially mean spreading the cost over time, in return for interest or a fee that goes to the finance company.

All finance companies from banks to specialist providers will conduct background checks on your business to be sure that you are capable of making the repayments. They usually need to view records of sales, turnover and expenditure as well as profit-and-loss accounts. Some will ask that you meet them in person to discuss requirements and eligibility.

Here are a few options:

## Bank loan

A standard bank loan might be the best option for a few reasons. The first is that banks often offer competitive rates of interest that won't vastly increase the unit price of the vehicle. Secondly, you probably have an existing relationship with a bank and may have agreed some kind of finance package with them in the past. Thirdly, there could be room to negotiate on your deal if you are a good customer that the bank values. This is especially true if you regularly borrow money to invest and have an excellent track record of timely repayments.

Of course, you don't have to settle for your existing bank. Shopping around might uncover better deals and you might be able to take advantage of special introductory offers or other incentives from rival institutions that want your business.

"My only loan was the purchase of my van and its sign writing. My bank supported me in the money and a small local company (TT Signs) took my ideas and produced a van to be proud of."

**– Jane Pennock, Us Girls Decorating Ltd**

## Motor company branded finance

Commercial vehicle brands usually offer their own packages, often managed by a third-party finance supplier. This will come with a range of incentives designed to compete with the banks.

Dealing direct with the manufacturer has its advantages. For example, you could negotiate a discount on the list price in return for a package, especially if you need to acquire more than one vehicle at once. The deal might include free insurance and maintenance packages, options on the term, free vehicle disposal and a flexible contract that can be extended if needed.

## Specialist vehicle finance

The benefit of specialist companies is the range of different deals they offer. You could go for hire purchase, which spreads payments and means you can keep the vehicle after all the instalments are completed.

A 'sale and lease back' arrangement means the provider buys your existing vehicle and finances it back to you, while leasing – in which you rent the vehicle and don't have to buy it – brings flexibility and eases the burden on cash flow. This latter option can be tax efficient because your vehicles don't show up as assets on your balance sheet.

As you can see, there are plenty of options to choose from, so shop around and always keep in mind the unique needs of your business, now and in the future.

## *Fitting out your van*

We all know that a van is essentially a powerful car with a large box on the back, but kitting it out with storage solutions will transform it into an efficient and convenient business asset. Larger vans – sometimes called 'Luton vans' – often come with tie rails that allow removals companies to secure furniture and stop it rattling around during transit.

In some cases these are also designed to incorporate metal shelving and racking. A quick online search will reveal the options, which offer varying degrees of capacity and segmentation. You can also get these designed on a custom basis and a number of companies will be happy to provide a quote for your specific needs.

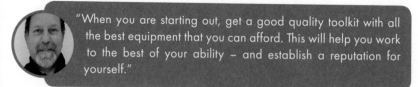

"When you are starting out, get a good quality toolkit with all the best equipment that you can afford. This will help you work to the best of your ability – and establish a reputation for yourself."

**– Wayne de Wet, Wayne de Wet Painting and Decorating Services**

# CHAPTER SIX

*Taking on Employees and Building Your Team*

"Taking people on might seem risky, but by recruiting well and at the right time, new employees will build your business for you."

**A**ccording to the Federation of Small Businesses (FSB) there were 5.7m businesses trading in the UK during 2017, a whopping 2.2m increase on the year 2000. The vast majority – some 99.3% – of these were small, and while small and medium businesses accounted for about 60% of total private sector employment, 4.3m businesses employed no one apart from the owners.

It means that more than three quarters of all the businesses in the UK are one-person affairs, either sole traders or limited companies with just a single person doing the work.

At the time of writing, 1.42m UK adults are unemployed, according to the Office for National Statistics. Using a bit of simple maths, if a third of sole traders took on a single member of staff they could eradicate unemployment entirely.

> "A key element in growing our business so quickly is offering people a probationary period of employment. If we have the wrong person in a particular role then it can affect the whole business negatively. As owners we have to be pretty ruthless and let people go if they are not going to be an asset to the business. A weak link in the chain is not good for the team."

*– Alan Gough, Warmglow Home Improvements Ltd*

The rise of self-employment has been driven by better technology, the price of which has fallen dramatically since the dotcom era of the late 1990s and early 2000s. The government's work to remove red tape and encourage business has contributed, as has the higher public profile of entrepreneurs thanks to successful TV shows like *Dragons' Den* and *The Apprentice*.

This 'perfect storm' of positive factors helped to create a wave of start-ups which the government hoped would gradually transform into the big international businesses of the future. It has worked to a degree but, as the stats show, there is still a reluctance among the overwhelming majority of business owners to build up by recruiting top talent.

Taking people on is a risk and a financial outlay that can feel like a major leap, but by recruiting well and at the right time, new employees will build your business for you.

> "Taking on employees is tricky. Finding the right candidate can be hard work and you may employ a few on a short-term basis before finding one who is right for you and the company. Always give them a probationary period, that way you get a chance to see how they work and make sure they are the sort of worker you need before committing to taking them full-time."

**– Matt Merry, Matt Merry Roofing**

This chapter looks at the pros and cons of growing beyond sole trader status and how to reduce the risk of taking on new employees, while magnifying the many potential rewards of bringing new skills and approaches into your venture. It also covers managing a team, keeping people motivated and what, if any, alternatives there are to recruitment when it comes to growing a business.

# SHOULD YOU TAKE ON STAFF?

Should you take on staff? Clearly, the answer to this question will depend on your unique circumstances, your goals and plans for the future. The small business figures from the FSB and Office for National Statistics suggest that a large number of sole traders are content with the flexibility and freedom that working for yourself brings.

Being a sole trader means there's no boss breathing down your neck and no one for whom you are responsible, so you can get on with the projects unrestricted by HR or management-related headaches.

A drawback of hiring your first member of staff is that, from the moment they sign on the dotted line, you have to shift at least some of your focus from fee-earning work to managing and taking care of your new employee or employees.

A huge benefit, however, is that each individual you add will bring new talents and experience. As your headcount grows so does your creativity, problem-solving capabilities and skillset. It's not just about raw people power – a team is usually greater than the sum of its parts.

> "Spend time thinking about what you need and take into account personality as well as skills. We've had some very talented people over the years who weren't team players. We've also had some less-qualified people that have turned into star employees because they're willing to learn."
>
> **– Adam Allsop, *The Shutter Studio Ltd***

If you created a sales strategy like the example outlined in chapter 4, you should have a very precise direction for your business as well as a clear idea of how you will achieve its goals. This, hopefully, will also tell you whether headcount needs to grow.

If you haven't created a strategy, don't fret, you can quickly weigh up the pros and cons of taking people on. Here's a quick (and by no means exhaustive) list of both; you might like to add your own based on your situation:

## *Pros*

- Employees bring new skills and ideas to the table.
- You can complete jobs faster, potentially increasing revenue.
- With staff it is possible to tackle more than one project simultaneously.

- Staff can provide good company and their development can provide you with a valuable legacy.

- As employees learn, they will be able to contribute more, delivering increased returns.

- Employees are essential to building a big business.

## *Cons*

- The new salary will hit your bottom line.

- You have to allocate time to management considerations – so, more paperwork.

- It might mean spending money on equipment, uniforms and training.

- A poor hiring decision could cost your business.

- Personality clashes can lead to lower productivity.

- Recruits might see you as a stepping stone to 'something bigger'.

The good news is that many of the cons can be ironed out with a grown-up approach to recruitment. A thorough, open-minded strategy based on the business's key requirements will vastly increase the chances of securing employees that make a big net contribution.

"It's important to employ people. I used to have business meetings with David Cameron and George Osborne at Number 10. They were very keen on boosting the economy and for entrepreneurs to help themselves by employing people.

"It doesn't matter how many – one, two or three – you have to start somewhere. The more people you employ, the better your chances of becoming a successful business, because you have more good people around you. You can start with an apprentice or a part-timer. There's no way I could have a business like I have today without help from others, it's just an impossibility."

**– Charlie Mullins, Pimlico Plumbers**

# THE JOB DESCRIPTION

If you decide to go for it and take on a member of staff, your first action should be to create a job description. This will cover all the areas of your business that require additional labour – and it should provide scope to grow as the business does.

It's useful to write the description down, not just to crystallise the details in your mind, but also to form the backbone of the job specification that you will be sending out to potential candidates.

The job description should define the position clearly, without stretching it out into an endless list of responsibilities. Set a rate of pay, not too much, not too little but enough to attract and retain an employee with the skillset you require.

Consider, too, whether any special qualifications are required. Should they have a certain level of driving licence, a certificate to use a piece of specialist equipment or a higher-level trade qualification? Try to cover these in your initial thought process so you can target people accurately.

> "We employ a labourer and a couple of regular subcontractors. We also use agency staff. Generally, when I find a pleasant guy who can complete the job well, I tend to keep their details. I am also always on site, so if we use agency staff, I can normally give a less competent decorator a job to do. This is probably the biggest advantage of me being on site, as I am able to pace workers according to their ability."

> **– Chris Jones, LSW Decorating Ltd**

Once your general description is finished, you're ready to write a job advertisement. A job ad should basically be a highlights package of your general job description; it should be snappy, inviting and aim to attract the right sort of attention.

When writing the advert it's important to remember some golden rules:

- People reading the ad will be hearing about your company and the vacancy for the first time, so make all the information simple and clear.

- Remember to state not just what the job involves, but also the calibre of desired candidates. In other words, explain what experience, qualifications and soft skills they should bring to the table.

- Ask them to include details of activities outside work in applications. This gives useful information about character traits and social skills.

- Consider how many people you want to respond to a job ad. One tactic is to play down the skill level and attract a wider haul of candidates. Another is to be more exacting, which risks an underwhelming response in terms of numbers but the calibre could be higher.

- Include essential information like the business address, contact number, deadline for applications, brand elements that convey the personality of the business and details of how to reply.

- Make your ad stand out. A striking, sparing design will help draw eyeballs to your job vacancy if it is competing with lots of others – for example, if it's positioned in a trade publication.

A job advert is a form of marketing and you have options as to where you should publish it. Local publications and websites might provide the best return, but you could also place adverts – with permission – in local colleges. This latter option is particularly useful if you plan to take on an apprentice; more on that later in this chapter.

# RECRUITING FOR THE FIRST TIME AND THE LAW

As well as the strategic approach to hiring your first employee, there are a series of legal obligations enshrined in UK law. According to Gov.uk, there are seven vital steps to hiring within the law:

1. Decide how much you are prepared to pay, noting that this figure can't fall below the National Minimum Wage (which varies depending on a person's age). Many companies sign up to the more generous 'living wage', which is calculated to equal basic monthly expenditure.

2. Check your candidates' legal right to work in the UK. Hiring illegal immigrants is against the law – regardless of whether you treat them well – and your business could be prosecuted if it breaks this rule.

3. Investigate whether your recruits have a criminal record and run a DBS check (formerly known as a CRB check), particularly if your work brings you into contact with children, vulnerable adults or security installations.

4. Get insured. It's likely you already have insurance to cover your work, customers and members of the public, but you need employers' liability insurance as soon as you take someone on as an employee.

5. Put the terms of employment in writing and send a copy to your new recruit to sign. If you're employing someone on a permanent basis (for one month or more) then you must provide them with a written job description that you both agree on.

6. Register as an employer with HM Revenue and Customs (HMRC). You'll need to declare your new status up to four weeks before you write your first paycheque.

7. Work out whether you have to provide a basic workplace pension under the government's auto-enrolment scheme. Most employers are now covered by this legislation, so it's likely you will have to sign up.

# HIRING AN APPRENTICE

"Joining Checkatrade has boosted my business and has now enabled me to take on my first employee, an apprentice school leaver. In September they will be going on a college apprenticeship for floor and wall tiling.

"This is an extremely exciting time for me and my new apprentice. Taking on my first employee is a big step, but if all goes to plan then in two years I'll do the same again!"

**– Simon Pitham, SEP Tiling Ltd**

For hundreds of years, young people have kick-started their careers with an apprenticeship. The combination of on-the-job learning and professional development is a win-win and is the secret of apprenticeships' enduring appeal.

Modern apprenticeships are more structured than the informal working relationships of yesterday, but the essential exchange of knowledge and labour remains the same. Today, it's a great way to make your first steps as an employer and to develop an employee with your vision for business.

Apprenticeships are a key pillar of the government's strategy for employment, which means there's plenty of help to get you started. If you're based in England, for example, you can apply for public funding to reimburse some of the costs of training your apprentice.

"We took an apprentice so we could train them the way we want them to work. We could teach customer service skills, how to be professional and leave a lasting impression so that customers use us again. We invested time, effort and money into our first apprentice just over a year ago and we are now reaping the rewards.

"We have an employee who works the way we want and is happy and willing. We have taken a couple of contracts on, knowing we have the time to be able to cover the work with additional employees. The next move is to recruit someone else!"

**– Jordan Williams, JR Williams Plumbing Services Ltd**

# SUCCESS STORIES ||||▶

**Name:** Jordan Williams
**Business name:** JR Williams Plumbing Services
**Type of business:** Plumbing and heating
**Number of employees:** 3

### How did you get started in your trade?

"I was working as a steel-pipe fitter in pressurised-cylinder refurbishment. It was physical, which I enjoyed, but incredibly boring so I decided to look elsewhere. I applied for a trainee plumber position thinking I had no chance. I then spent a few years at college to learn the trade."

### Has the business changed since you started?

"More and more people are going online or getting word-of-mouth recommendations. Online reviews and a digital presence is one of the most important things now. Replying to reviews is essential. No matter how big you grow, each customer wants to feel special. You need to make them feel unique."

### Describe your typical customer and project.

"That's what I love about this job: there isn't one. Some customers want a supply only, so they know exactly what the labour costs are; some want guidance and some want to not get involved at all.

"Gas work is usually the area where I have to advise and guide the customer but we are seeing more and more on the bathroom side of things. Being a plumber is no longer enough – customers don't want to have to bring several tradespeople in, they want one who sorts the whole project."

### What do you enjoy about your career?

"When a customer pays me with a smile on their face, I know I did that. When a customer can turn the water back on, have heating again or finally have the power shower they always wanted, it's because I did it. The gratitude some customers give you, when they can't thank you enough, makes all the horrible jobs forgettable."

### What's the hardest thing about it, or the biggest challenge you face?

"Rogue tradesmen and VAT registration. We pride ourselves on being Chartered, Gas Safe, WIAPS-approved along with several other accreditations. These cost money which needs to be recovered somewhere. The customer is at ease, knowing that you are reputable – but of course it comes at a cost. Most don't mind the slight increase. However, you will lose a few jobs because the unlicensed guy down the road will do it a bit cheaper."

### What are your plans for the future?

"To aim bigger. We have learnt several valuable lessons along the way. We've had contracts we had to terminate due to other poor performing companies and our aim is to get involved with bigger, more reputable companies. Also, we want to educate the public through our advertising and social media platforms that paying a little more for the right tradesman means you don't have to pay again."

### What's your best tip for other tradespeople in your sector?

"If you're a tradesperson, you already have the ability to do your job well. That aside, customers need to be kept informed; communicate with them and be open and honest. It's not about your qualifications, it's about you as a person.

"Some of our customers have told us that we got the job because of our approach, not our price. Show them respect – it's their home. Give them informed choices and, above all, keep them updated with dates, times and costs!"

There are also some rules covering apprentices that in many ways go beyond normal employment rules. These are mainly there to protect young people and ensure they see the benefits of learning and development. So, apprentices must:

- be at least 16 years old
- learn work skills
- mix with experienced staff and not just do menial work
- study at college or a training centre during the working week
- receive at least the minimum wage for their age group.

Apprenticeships can be given to new recruits or existing staff and they can last anywhere between one and five years, depending on the level and type of qualification that your recruit is going for. You'll need to pick a framework or standard for an apprenticeship, choose a training organisation, check funding offers and, once you have found your apprentice, create an apprenticeship agreement and commitment statement.

Working with an apprenticeship service makes these steps easier – and if necessary they will help advertise the position and connect you with potential candidates. For more details, contact the National Apprenticeship Service.

> "I knew we couldn't employ a qualified plumber so decided to build slowly and took an apprentice. We took the financial hit of his wages from our profit line, but you have to sacrifice things to enable yourself to grow.
>
> "The reason we decided to do this was because I was receiving around ten calls a week for the small jobs but I had to turn them all down due to me fitting a bathroom or heating system. We now have two vehicles so when we are on large jobs I can send my employee to do the smaller jobs. This gets us in the door of a lot of properties and we have a high conversion rate of small jobs to bigger jobs within the same properties.
>
> "We pay above the national living wage and regularly buy lunch, coffee and allow him to keep scrap and tips as we believe happy staff are productive staff. We are now putting things in place to take someone else on – this time, probably qualified."
>
> **– Jordan Williams, JR Williams Plumbing Services Ltd**

## The Enterprise Trust

Founded by Richard Harpin in 2011 and run by Helen Booth, the Enterprise Trust is a charity focused on supporting young people to achieve more than they ever thought possible. Richard was 15 years old when he started his first business and has a passion for inspiring young people to set up and run their own business.

Richard has committed £1m a year of his personal income to the Enterprise Trust over the next eight years to support young people across the country to become entrepreneurs and to create a legacy of independent wealth generators.

The charity funds programmes that support young people to come up with an enterprising idea, improve their entrepreneurial skills and become their own boss. Already, within the first year of operation, there is evidence of individuals attending the workshops and gaining the confidence to create business plans and start their own businesses. The first step can even be a 'side hustle' outside of studies or work that leads to a prosperous future.

Developing the right skills is critical and the Enterprise Trust works in partnership with leading national apprenticeship providers to encourage more young people to complete an apprenticeship in the trade sector. A good apprentice will be a valuable asset to any business and the charity is committed to encouraging employers to take on an apprentice to reap these benefits.

The Enterprise Trust has also sponsored the author of this book, producing good quality advice and guidance for individuals who have the passion and drive to grow their own business and go for it!

# BUILDING AND MANAGING A TEAM

It's one thing to recruit a bunch of people, it's another to build a team.

A team is a group of individuals who work together to get a project finished, helping, encouraging and leading each other as they go. Creating a bond and a spirit of community is important: it makes people come to work because they want to, not because they have to. This adds up to a higher standard of work and more happy customers.

It's not an easy job to create a workforce that is enthused, engaged and eager to get the job done. A positive company culture takes a series of steps to get going, followed by constant revisiting – and if necessary tinkering – to keep people operating at their full potential.

The first steps to creating a team were talked about earlier: step one is hiring great people who are a solid fit for your business (covered earlier in this chapter). Step two is involving them in the development of your vision and strategy (see chapter 4); teams are more engaged if they understand the why as well as the what, where and when.

> "I employed women for two years, but I struggled to pay the bills. One cannot pay low wages for a strenuous job and again cannot increase the daily rate to an unreasonable amount. Unfortunately, I had to stop this support. All the women supported the image of my company, they worked hard and respected learning how to do things my way."

**– Jane Pennock, Us Girls Decorating Ltd**

Further elements in developing a winning team include strong leadership, communication, training, delegating, instilling values and fast and effective conflict resolution. Let's address each in turn:

## Leadership

The best leaders build relationships through trust and respect, which in turn breeds loyalty. A healthy respect for the boss is a good thing, but not if it tips over into fear and resentment. So, it's important to curb your temper, even when things go wrong, and be constructive with people.

It'll help if you have a clear and simple idea of the business's values and goals, which you can mentally refer back to each time you need to provide some direction. It's hard to offer guidance if you aren't completely sure yourself, so set your standards and be prepared to share them.

Ground rules could be as simple as ensuring people turn up on time, or dress appropriately, or behave well. These simple directives give your team an identity that will increase their sense of pride and help to distinguish your business from the competition.

## Communication

Communication is one of the most important factors in creating successful businesses. People should want to listen, and when they do they should receive regular messages that are practical and easy to understand.

The bigger your workforce, the simpler the message has to be. No one should be left confused, so clarify points, particularly if you need people to act on them quickly and decisively. Be prepared to hear ideas and don't try to be the sole creative force behind the business. Popular leaders are great communicators, but they are also good listeners.

So encourage discussion, because it could lead to ideas that generate new revenue, shave away costs or improve customer satisfaction. If you reassure your team that there's no such thing as a stupid idea, you'll be rewarded with a lot of good ones.

That doesn't mean arranging lots of meetings, just being open to suggestions. Ask for views, give them your attention and respond constructively whether you think ideas are good or bad.

## Training

People don't just do a job for the money, they also want to learn skills and become better at what they do. Even motivated workers can become jaded over time if they don't feel they are making progress or learning anything new.

This is where training comes in. By offering semi-regular opportunities to learn new skills, you'll maintain higher levels of staff engagement, loyalty and morale. Of course, there are always opportunities to learn on the job, particularly for younger workers, but the prospect of professional accreditations and qualifications are a real perk for new recruits and long-term employees alike.

## Delegating

Delegating is one of the hardest aspects of growing a business, but it's also a great way to grow and motivate your team. Granted, it feels strange to give someone else decision-making responsibility when you have worked so hard to build the venture according to your own values.

But in a successful business it quickly becomes impossible to manage everything and you'll need to cede power to others. The good news is that this is a great morale boost for your senior team. Showing that you trust them is a real motivator and in most cases they will repay you with carefully considered decisions.

## Instilling values

They say that company culture starts at the top, so use your (well-rehearsed) standards to set the tone. Encourage staff to cooperate on projects and challenge them to follow your lead. A great team is not just about your relationship with staff, but also their relationships with each other, so encourage trust and respect in all directions.

## Conflict resolution

Note that managing people is a two-way street and it's not just about what you think or how you feel, but the thoughts and feelings of team members. Emotional intelligence is an asset in business, regardless of your industry, so be on the lookout for warning signs in people's moods and intervene positively if things start to sour.

Remember also that minor disputes will erupt naturally from time to time and that your role should be as a mediator and problem-solver. Deal with mole hills before they become mountains and don't get bogged down taking sides in the nitty-gritty of the dispute – to do so is a waste of time.

# OUTSOURCING

There are many benefits to recruiting staff and building teams, but the downsides of cost, time and energy are too much for some business owners. If this applies to you then an alternative way to grow your business is through outsourcing.

Specialist companies in areas from marketing and finance to admin and secretarial services are available to take on the non-core work you don't have time for. On top of this, many small businesses subcontract work to other companies operating in the same industry. This is often the case with smaller jobs where the original company pays the subcontractor for work delivered while taking a finder's fee for themselves.

Outsourcing is a flexible way to take on more projects and can be a useful stopgap while you start to recruit a team. The downside is you must put your trust in a team you have little control over; the quality of their work and the way they approach the job will reflect on your business, whether it's good or bad.

"Having previously employed fitters and very nearly losing everything over it, we reverted back to having all our fitters subcontracted. We have found good ways to find and retain fitters, but finding management staff, which we have a current need for, is definitely an ongoing struggle.

"The move from one-man band to a larger company is hard, and finding my number two, short of the invention of cloning, is something that still eludes me!"

**– Chris Fairbairn, Cribbit Installations Ltd**

# CHAPTER SEVEN

*Dealing with Money*

"Money is the lifeblood of any business. Getting the numbers right is essential."

They say that cash is king and it's certainly true that money is the lifeblood of any business, whether a start-up or a multi-national corporation. Getting the numbers right is essential, because even very successful businesses with large revenues have come unstuck because cash wasn't in the bank when it was needed.

Money is also the mark of success in business: if there's more coming in than going out, it's cause for celebration. The reverse is cause for a return to the drawing board.

But there are numerous other ways in which companies are impacted by money, whether it's getting paid on time or moving money on to HMRC in the form of corporation tax, VAT, National Insurance contributions or capital gains tax.

You need to carefully manage cash flow, payroll, surpluses and debts in such a way that your business is free to grow without being weighed down by financial considerations. This chapter is all about organising your cash so it works for you and not against you.

*Don't forget the great finance apps we looked at in chapter 5 when discussing tech and systems that can help you. (See page 79 onwards.)*

"I ensure all potential customers are aware of my daily rate and that a long job can reach a four-figure amount during my initial visit. To support this my final written estimates are very detailed. It gives the customer confidence because they know specifically what I will work on. It also acts as my job sheet.

"Ninety to 95% of my jobs have been completed within my estimated time frame. Ensuring that the calendar is full of work means that I can pay my bills, including to our dear HMRC!"

**– Jane Pennock, Us Girls Decorating Ltd**

# SUCCESS STORIES ||||⬛⬛➡

**Name:** Jane Pennock
**Business name:** Us Girls Decorating
**Type of business:** Painting and decorating
**Number of employees:** 1

### How did you get started in your trade?

"I got started with a change of career. I spent 23 years in retail as a designer with a clothing company. Towards the end I set up an office at home and started working for myself remotely. At the same time, I set up a small company for painting and decorating – just for small jobs just to keep me going. It went from there."

### Has the business changed since you started?

"I have learned a lot since setting up the business. I grew in confidence with wallpapering and my work in general. I didn't go to evening classes, so these were life skills."

### Describe your typical customer and project.

"My typical customers are households. It's only me, so I stick to local jobs which I can do really well. I turn away work which is too big, it's important to be honest about that."

### What do you enjoy about your career?

"It's a hard slog going through it on your own, but then you see the end product, which is incredibly fulfilling. You can see how much it means to people when you have done a great job for them."

### What's the hardest thing about it, or the biggest challenge you face?

"Trying to grow the business is hard. I employed someone for a time and the cost is quite high, because it's manual work and you can't pay a pittance. Teaching the skills while working on the job is tricky. You have to tick all the right boxes legally, which takes time, yet you can't raise your prices to account for that."

### What are your plans for the future?

"I just want to keep doing good work and see more smiling faces at the end of each job. I love going the extra mile and even tidying up work that other tradespeople have left in a mess. It's very satisfying."

### What's your best tip for other tradespeople in your sector?

"The customer comes first. You are in their home so treat them the way you want to be treated. Don't go home leaving a dirty workplace behind you! Make it livable. Be a good communicator, but also show them that you care."

# GETTING PAID

You can't manage your money if there's nothing in your bank account, so getting paid is the first step to financial peace of mind. Sadly, payment is a prickly issue for small businesses and late or non-payment is responsible for thousands of business insolvencies each year.

According to research firm Dun & Bradstreet, the average small or medium-sized business is owed £63,881 in late payments. Its survey of 500 companies with between two and 250 employees found that 35% of them had cash flow problems as a result.

Just over 10% were owed between £100,000 and £250,000, while a whopping 51% said the problem of late payment was getting worse. Most seriously of all, almost six in ten respondents said it was putting their business at risk of failure.

> "People weren't paying on time so we adopted a policy of charging a material cost of 10% at the start of the job. An invoice is then sent out with payment due within five days. A gentle reminder is then sent out as a prompt.
>
> "I feel it is important to have a professional, properly drawn up policy. This is an area that we are currently looking into, including subcontractors' terms and conditions, privacy policy, payment terms, acceptance of work contract and employment contracts."

**– Chris Jones, LSW Decorating Ltd**

Officially, businesses that are owed money can claim interest and charge for debt recovery costs if payment isn't forthcoming within a set period of time. But few businesses invoke the law because they don't want to sour relationships with treasured customers.

So if legal action isn't an option for you, what are the alternatives? Good payment practice can increase your chances of being paid on time and reduce the impact of late payment on your business.

# 1. Be clear about your terms from the start

It's tempting to ignore the practicalities of payment just after you have won a juicy contract. But being clear and transparent (in a friendly way) about how and when you'd like to be paid increases your chances of a positive outcome.

# 2. Invoice ASAP

Too many small businesses are laid back about invoicing. It's important to submit invoices at the earliest possible opportunity instead of giving a customer an easy excuse to delay settlement. That could mean filing before work is completed, especially if you have invested money in a project and payment terms are 30 days or more.

Always accompany an early invoice with an explanation that reassures the customer, such as *"I'm popping this over while I remember"* or *"I'm doing the company accounts and wanted to ensure you got this on time"* or *"I just wanted you to have this in the system, no need to settle early"*.

Many organisations have arbitrary payment schedules, meaning that if you write 30 days on your invoice, payment will arrive in 30 days regardless whether it is submitted early or six months late. Handing an invoice in early means the ball is in their court, not yours.

> "I approach every job in a professional manner, which means customers understand that I want them to act in a similar way when it comes to paying me on time. I introduce payment terms early on, even before we have agreed on the job during the consultation phase, because then they understand the terms and are far more likely to stick to them."

**– Wayne de Wet, Wayne de Wet Painting and Decorating Services**

# 3. Calculate costs on the fly

By keeping a running total of your costs while carrying out the work, it'll be easy to add them in when the time comes to invoice. Trying to remember everything at the end, plus adding it all up, just increases the time it takes to get your invoice out the door.

## 4. Invest in a card payment machine

In the modern world of electronic payments, cash is slipping down the pecking order as a preferred way to settle bills. People are increasingly turning to card payments – including contactless ones.

A great way to ensure you get paid on time more regularly is to offer card payment services at the end of a project. This is particularly useful for smaller domestic jobs lasting up to a day. The service isn't complicated and a growing number of tech companies offer simple card readers without the need to take on a merchant account or an expensive PDQ (process data quickly) machine rental.

iZettle is one member of this new breed. At the time of writing you can pick up an easy-to-use card reader, incorporating contactless and mobile payments, for under £30 and it simply charges 1.75% for every card transaction you put through.

iZettle competes with companies like Square (a US-based company that recently extended to the UK), SumUp, PayPal Here and WorldPay Zinc. Each option comes with its own pluses, minuses and different fee structure. Have a look around and see what's best for your business.

## 5. Don't make mistakes on invoices

An invoice contains a lot of precise and important information, so it's not surprising that errors occasionally creep in. It's a real pain for all sides when a customer comes to pay an invoice but has to go back to the supplier and ask for details to be fixed.

A good invoice includes the following (accurate) information:

- business name, logo, registered address and company number
- your customer's name and address (make sure the name quoted is the person paying)

- details of the service (or products) you have supplied
- if applicable, a purchase order number or related reference
- the amount due and the date it should be paid by (and the date the invoice is being sent)
- VAT details, if you are registered (remember to add 20% to the bill)
- payment options.

Ensure that all these points are written clearly and accurately, because a mistake anywhere could lead to a delay.

# 6. Follow up

Don't let a customer put your invoice to the back of their mind. It's generally a good idea to schedule a friendly reminder over email if your payment terms have elapsed and money is not forthcoming. Again, adopt a friendly tone. It's possible that a clerical error has caused the delay and that the customer has no qualms about paying. You could try something like the following:

> *Dear _____*
>
> *Thanks again for the contract. The team really enjoyed working with you on the project and we're keen to do so again in future.*
>
> *Would you mind checking with your accounts team to see if our invoice is going through OK? Am sure everything is on track, but I wanted to circle back just in case it has been mislaid.*
>
> *All the best,*
>
> *_____*

It's perfectly acceptable to give someone a nudge in this way and 99% of customers will respond positively, perhaps even apologetically, when they realise they are late. Keep the conversation going until the money is safely in the bank and don't threaten punitive action unless you absolutely have to.

# MANAGING CASH FLOW

Maintaining cash flow is one of the trickier aspects of running a business, especially if much of the trade is seasonal. You have to balance boom months with lean times and ensure that bills are settled and salary commitments are met.

One of the best ways to ensure money flows thick and fast through your bank account is to follow the advice above on invoicing best practice. But there are a few other useful methods besides being timely with payment demands.

## *Focus on cash flow*

Cash flow is subtly different to sales or profits and it could be argued that ignoring the latter in favour of the former will shore up your business as it grows. Cash flow refers to money arriving in your bank account, something that isn't guaranteed with a sale. People celebrate a signature on a purchase order, but really those celebrations should be postponed until the money is in their hands.

If income is patchy and you don't feel that payments are coming in a reliable pattern, save a war chest of (ideally) three months' salaries. This will take pressure off the constant money flow and will provide a much-needed reserve if, for whatever reason, there's a dry spell.

## *Set a cash flow forecast*

It's surprising how much easier it is to steer your business away from financial trouble if you understand what money is coming in and going out in the next six months. Predicting your finances, based on credits and debits now and in the future, brings clarity to the question of whether you can spend or should save to avoid hot water down the line.

## Make payments as easy as possible

Gone are the days when cash-in-hand was the default method of payment for tradespeople. But more to the point, you'll need to give some options to customers if you want your business to grow. Electronic payments are best because there's a clear record of payment and no chance – unlike with cash or cheques – that money will be lost in transit to the bank.

Better yet, if you're in a position to do so, offer fixed-term payment packages delivered from the customer's account via a standing order or direct debit. This method is especially relevant to businesses with a service involving regular upkeep, such as cleaners and gardeners.

You could come up with a list of three itemised packages, each at a different price point and listing exactly what the customer will get and when in each case. Combine this with your customer relationship management (CRM) system to fill your schedule with regular dependable appointments and payments.

## Use technology

The digital revolution makes cash flow management much easier than the old days of spreadsheets and pencils. The Cloud helps businesses handle information across teams. It means information (financial information in this case) can be updated in one place and viewed by someone in a different location, presuming they have access to the software. The facts and figures are updated for everyone, everywhere.

People no longer have to store information all in one place and go there to access it. This saves time and enables teams to work faster and keep a closer eye on finances, even from a smartphone.

## Keep the bank onside

It's true that banking relationships aren't what they used to be. Gone are the days when a business could expect to see the same friendly faces every time they visited their bank manager. But this doesn't mean relationships are no longer important.

Banks, along with all other public-facing institutions, keep a record of their dealings with customers. Calls are often recorded, but more importantly every time you make a request or seek a change to your banking setup, information will be added to your file.

Banks love communication and they particularly appreciate being kept in the loop when customers start to get into difficulties. By keeping up the conversation, you'll inspire trust in your banking provider and they will be more likely to help (maybe with a loan or overdraft facility) if cash flow issues arise.

## Give someone responsibility for the numbers

For extra financial security, train a member of staff to monitor incoming and outgoing payments and to report back regularly, especially if there is cause for concern. By allocating the role and providing training, you can reduce the risk of falling into the red while providing a valued employee with additional responsibility.

"To help customers pay, we have secured backing from Barclays bank to offer finance packages."

*– Alan Gough, Warmglow Home Improvements Ltd*

# ACCOUNTANCY AND TAX

Tax is never a popular part of doing business, but along with paperwork it is a reality that all entrepreneurs must face. As you no doubt already know, tax is money taken by the government each time a transaction occurs; how much tax is paid depends on a complex system of variables.

There are various forms of tax affecting people and businesses – and these levies must be paid periodically throughout the year, otherwise you'll start to receive red letters through the door and, ultimately, visits from a bailiff.

The simplest tax structure is reserved for sole traders who haven't incorporated into limited businesses. These 'freelancers' simply charge a fee, accept payment into a bank account and then calculate how much tax they need to pay at the end of each year.

But it doesn't take much for the tax picture to become a lot more complicated. Growth, recruitment, profits and value added tax (VAT) registration all have a major impact. Here are some of the most common taxes a business might have to deal with:

- **Corporation tax:** Paid on business profits. There are different rates for small and big businesses – the rates change frequently.
- **VAT:** Businesses qualifying for VAT must charge 20% on all invoices and pass the money on to HMRC on a quarterly basis. In many cases businesses can claim VAT on purchases back from the Treasury.
- **Income tax:** Paid by individuals on income derived from salaries. In most cases the tax is lifted from pay packets before employees receive them.
- **National Insurance:** Paid by workers and employers to help fund state benefits, most notably the state pension. Employees have to earn above a certain threshold before they start paying.
- **Capital gains:** Affects transactions in which someone makes a profit on the purchase price or cost of the thing being sold. Business owners pay capital gains when they sell a business to another party.
- **Dividends tax:** Paid by directors of companies who choose to remunerate themselves via dividends instead of or as well as via a salary. Dividends tax is also paid by investors on sales of stocks, shares and bonds etc.

Because of the variety of taxes out there, plus the fact that many apply differently to different types of businesses, it's often a good idea to engage the services of a tax professional or business adviser. Their job is to make sense of it all so you don't have to.

# HIRING AN ACCOUNTANT

People often start businesses intending to do everything themselves. They think, quite rightly, that keeping costs down in the early days will give the business a better chance of long-term success. But then reality dawns. Many realise that crunching their own numbers is a false economy that costs more than it saves.

Despite what the famous advert says, tax *can* be really quite taxing, especially if your business is complex and is registered for VAT, with lots of complicated equations involving salaries, debt and grants. It can be the cause of stress, anxiety and sleepless nights.

If you're currently working without the services of an accountant – in other words, if you're doing your own business and/or personal tax returns – then you're either a multi-talented and highly organised individual, or you're spending a lot of time searching for documents, working out complex sums and toing and froing with HMRC.

In the latter case, it's almost certainly worth investigating hiring an accountant. The golden rule is that if you can earn the cost of accountancy services doing a job that you understand and enjoy, then it's time to give up the calculator.

Accountants are specialists with tax and business planning in the same way you are with wiring, plumbing or fencing (or whatever your trade happens to be). They should have a good working relationship with HMRC and an extensive knowledge of the tax system.

A good accountant will assist your business in meeting all of its tax obligations (without suffering late filing or payment penalties) and can advise you on tax-deductible expenditure and tax incentives. In other words, you could reduce your tax exposure by running your finances in a certain way.

> "Have money behind you to start with and use an accountant. When starting a company you're not going to wake up one morning and be booked up for the next three months with more work coming in daily. That takes time and within the first couple of years you'll find times where you have no work at all.
>
> "If you've got money behind you this will help you through these times. If you have friends, family or people you know in the trade who are established then they might give you some work during quieter times.
>
> "Having an accountant to do your books and finances is the easiest way. Some of the forms you have to fill out for self assessments and the like can be very confusing. An accountant will ensure they are filled out properly to stop you getting into trouble with HMRC."

*– Matt Merry, Matt Merry Roofing*

So accountants are there to save you time, money and stress. The good news for small businesses is that you don't have to hire a professional in-house, because there is such a wide variety of outsourced options to choose from.

Companies as diverse as Crunch Accounting, KPMG, inniAccounts and hundreds more will help you run your books with fees ranging from £800 to £2,000 a year for a small business with simple tax liabilities – a fraction of what you would pay a bookkeeper.

> "Cash flow is difficult, but with the assistance of the bank, who have provided an overdraft to cover cash flow on larger projects, and a loan for investment in machinery to move the business forward, it is achievable.
>
> "I had very little personal money to invest in my business, but I now have nearly ten times the turnover than I did in the early years. I use an accountant for all tax affairs – my expertise is in kitchens and bathrooms, so my time is wasted if I try to do this side of things on my own."

*– Chris Fairbairn, Cribbit Installations Ltd*

# ACCOUNTANCY SOFTWARE

The arrival of 'fintech' (financial technology) has greatly improved the tech behind accountancy software. Paper and pens are out the window, replaced by cloud computing and inputting/uploading of invoices, expenses and payments at the touch of a button.

All of the accountancy services listed above come with software. Your job is to input invoices, payments and expenses; when it comes to paying the taxman, the software will do the necessary calculations and your accountant will check and file documents with HMRC.

The software is improving all the time. At the time of writing, a good software package will allow you to take a picture of a receipt for automatic expense filing and to send invoices via your smartphone as soon as you close your customer's door behind you.

The combination of smart technology and smart accountants is brilliant for businesses on the move. It allows you to spend a whole lot less time on taxes and instead focus on doing what you do best. It's possible to commission a tax specialist and get a subscription to accountancy software separately – in most cases this won't be a problem for either party.

# BORROWING MONEY

Borrowing money is normal in business, but it's important to borrow for the right reasons. Normally a finance provider like a bank will lend money to a business for a specific reason, such as to buy a vehicle or a piece of machinery.

In most cases, it won't lend money to cover salaries or other day-to-day outgoings. This is the origin of the old adage that people can only borrow money when they don't need to. However, at the start of your banking relationship it's a good idea to enquire about debt facilities like an overdraft. This might prove valuable as you invest to grow or fall into a temporary cash flow trap.

As with any product, loans are part of a market with different offers, charges and conditions attached. So it pays to shop around for the best deal, particularly if you plan to borrow a large amount of cash for a major capital investment, for example.

Given that money is money, it's surprising to see wildly different interest rates offered just by the major banks. But dig a little deeper and the range of loans broadens further. You might want to look at the British Business Bank, a state-owned company that lends to growing businesses, for example.

You could also consider peer-to-peer lending via services such as Zopa or RateSetter, which could offer easier access to finance, or you could go the old-fashioned route of falling back on family and friends for a small IOU.

Borrowing from the people you know has obvious advantages – for example, you don't have to go through the same affordability checks you would with a professional lender. But it also has drawbacks, as many a friendship has broken down over debt, so think hard before you go cap in hand.

# HOW TO SECURE EXTERNAL FUNDING
## *by Barclays*

Running a business can be exciting, especially when new growth opportunities come along, but it can be hard to know how to finance the next stage of development. If that's the case, external funding could provide a solution.

## At what point should I approach a bank?

The most critical piece of advice is to engage with your bank as early as possible.

Many businesses decide on a strategy and put a figure on the funding they require before contacting their lender. Sharing your ideas at an earlier stage allows your bank to better understand your strategic aims when the application for finance is submitted.

This approach requires you to have open conversations about plans that may not be fully formulated. However, early conversations can ensure all options are discussed, which should make you and lenders more comfortable when making future decisions.

## What do banks look for?

There's no method to guarantee success when pitching for business finance, but that doesn't mean you can't give yourself an advantage by presenting your case in the best possible way.

Many lenders, including Barclays, will use the CAMPARI framework to assess your application. If you can satisfy this model in your pitch for funding, you'll go a long way to getting a positive outcome. And don't forget to add in anything that makes your business stand out, for example if you've won awards or been particularly successful in a certain area. Think about whether there's anything relevant that the bank might not ask about but that could put your business in a stronger position.

- **C – Character:** This is your chance to shine, and in business financing terms that means convincing investors that you – and your business – have the professionalism to look after their money and give them a return. That can incorporate many things, from the confidence you have in your idea, to your business's record in making loan repayments. Having a strong brand reputation can go a long way.

- **A – Ability:** You need to show clearly that you and the people in your business have the knowledge and ability to generate growth from any funding that's provided. Your track record as a business is likely to be considered, as is the quality of its products or services and the strengths of the management team. Your staff could also play an important role – having good people in key positions helps to give lenders confidence, so consider taking on outside expertise if you need to bring additional expertise into the business.

- **M – Means:** Is your business equipped to deliver on your growth ambitions? This is where the strength of your business plan comes into action. You should try to show where you have, or will have, a competitive advantage in the market. You should also prepare detailed financial reports with best and worst-case scenarios, future growth projections, prior performance records and in-depth company expenditure.

- **P – Purpose:** Lenders will want to know what the money will be used for and how it will be used to generate a profit or improve the business's financial situation. This part of the framework is also where prospective investors will consider whether the borrowing is in the best interests of the business, whether there's a good enough reason for requesting it and whether it fits in with their own lending guidelines.

- **A – Amount:** How much are you asking for, and is it the right amount for your stated requirements? Potential investors will want to see how you have decided on the level of funding you are asking for, how it aligns with your financial projections and what the business's own contributions to the project may be. It's worth taking the time to scrutinise this properly. While it's a good idea to be prudent, asking for too little could be counterproductive if it means your plans are judged as being less likely to succeed.

- **R – Repayment:** You'll need to be able to show concrete evidence that you will be able to afford any repayments, or provide solid projections that indicate how you'll be able to pay back your investors over time. Lenders will be looking for details on the source of the repayment money and will likely be considering areas such as the health of your cash flow, your profit margins, and if the repayment period is acceptable.

- **I – Insurance:** In many cases it's important for you to be able to show that you have a fallback plan in case things go wrong. Do you have another source of repayment? Has any insurance been taken out that would allow you to repay the financing if you fall short of your targets? If you're securing the finance on an asset, make sure you have an up-to-date valuation to show.

In addition to the questions above, banks will also look for some specific financial information to help them assess your application.

## Up-to-date financial statements (created within nine months)

Information on how well the business has been performing in the recent past.

## Your business plan

A business plan will help you collate and clarify your business ideas, plan for the future of your business, and show whether your idea is realistic and workable. Your business plan will play a key role in attracting funding to get your business started, so you should make sure you have one prepared before applying for lending.

Think about how your new venture supports your long-term aims and the wider goals of your business. This will help the bank to understand how a new opportunity fits with your business strategy, structure and current operation.

## Forecasts of 12 months

In addition to historic and recent performance, your business plan should include realistic projections for the future. It can be useful to include a 'what if' analysis, demonstrating that you have considered the effect of events such as the unexpected loss of a key customer, increased competitive pressures or a rise in operating costs.

## Alternative funding solutions

Sometimes a bank isn't always the right source of funding, and there are a range of other options available to businesses.

- **Crowdfunding:** This is where businesses raise small amounts of money from lots of people, via specialist online platforms. In exchange for the cash, businesses can promise a range of things such as early access to products, discounts or equity stakes in the business. Crowdfunding can be used for purposes as diverse as funding a small project to getting a new business off the ground, but with many businesses fighting for attention it can be hard to successfully raise the money you might be looking for.

- **Peer-to-peer lending:** This combines aspects of traditional lending and crowdfunding together, with specialist online platforms allowing businesses to take out loans funded by many individual investors. The criteria for borrowing in this way can be less strict than traditional banks, while you may also be able to borrow more and get your hands on the cash more quickly. But costs are not always lower than they would be for a traditional business loan from a bank.

## Key takeaways

Engage with your bank as early as possible. Open conversations about your plans and financial requirements during business planning will help your bank to have a better understanding of your business when assessing a future funding application.

Consider the range of funding options so that you are confident you have chosen the appropriate solution for your business. Early discussions with your bank should support you in making this decision.

When applying for funding, you will be asked to provide up-to-date financial statements, forecasts, and a comprehensive business plan.

## *About Barclays*

Barclays is a transatlantic consumer and wholesale bank with global reach, offering products and services across personal, corporate and investment banking, credit cards and wealth management, with a strong presence in our two home markets of the UK and the US.

With over 325 years of history and expertise in banking, Barclays operates in over 40 countries and employs approximately 85,000 people. Barclays moves, lends, invests and protects money for customers and clients worldwide.

Visit **barclays.co.uk/business-banking** to find out more.

# CHAPTER EIGHT

*Keeping on Top of
Legal Stuff*

# "Complying with the law is an important aspect of growing a business."

**R**ed tape, along with tax, is consistently one of the top-ranking gripes for business owners everywhere. Form filling is time-consuming and distracting; most business owners see it as an unwanted interference with the more exciting job of making sales and completing projects.

But complying with the law is an important aspect of growing a business and the forms are there to ensure that employees and management are both safe, paying what they owe and operating in a fashion that's above board.

Rules apply in varying ways to different types of business and it's important to look into these factors as early as the start-up phase when you're thinking about the type of business you want to be. Business formats include sole trader, limited company, partnership, invested business (having shareholders brings with it more responsibilities) and public limited company (businesses listed on the stock market).

Assuming you're not quite ready for the FTSE 100 just yet, the most likely format for your business will be one of three options. So let's start at the beginning.

# SOLE TRADER

Sole trader, limited company and partnership are the three simplest forms of business and each comes with its own regulatory environment, tax treatment, challenges and opportunities. Most tradespeople are sole traders, mainly because it is a simple route into business that requires little formal paperwork and has straightforward tax obligations.

In broad terms, becoming a sole trader involves telling the tax authorities (HMRC again) that you are self-employed. In return you will receive a tax self-assessment form each year, in which you have to declare your business's revenue and work-related expenditure.

Your income, the difference between revenue and expenditure, will be taxed. How much tax you pay depends on how much money you clear after all costs are taken into consideration.

As a sole trader, you are the business. That means you are personally liable for financial losses, so if you somehow incur a £20,000 debt then it is your sole responsibility to pay it back. You will also need all the necessary insurance – for example, public liability – in order to work in homes and business premises.

Aside from these details you are free to operate as you wish. It is this level of freedom that has attracted around 4m people to become sole traders. You can even employ people in this format – as long as you fulfill all of the legal and moral obligations that comes with (see chapter 6) – and you can register for VAT.

But the system has a few drawbacks. One, as mentioned, is your complete personal exposure if the business suffers a loss. Sole traders have unlimited liability for debts or fines if they are unlucky enough to face legal action.

It can be harder to raise finance as a sole trader, because institutions like banks prefer the comparative safety of more formal business structures. And although sole traders enjoy simpler tax structures to other forms of business, that doesn't mean they pay less tax overall.

A further downside is the fact that business and personal finance often gets mixed up, which makes filling in an annual tax return more complicated – although admittedly this is easily fixed by setting up a separate business bank account.

Another downside is reputational. When people think of sole traders they conjure a different picture to that of an incorporated business. Generally speaking, the image of a limited company is professional, established, regulated and therefore perhaps a safer bet.

This isn't always the case in reality, and it's true that some customers prefer to work with sole traders because of the perceived informal, familiar approach, but this reputational element is worth some thought. How do you want to come across?

# LIMITED COMPANY

Unlike a sole trader, a limited company is an independent legal entity. 'Limited' is short for limited liability, which means the structure of the business is legally separated from the individual or individuals who run it.

Crucially, personal assets are not at risk if a limited company suffers losses, except in special circumstances (such as an owner arranging a bank loan secured against their home). The money you invest in growing your business is vulnerable if things go wrong, but nothing else.

Limited companies are taxed differently to sole traders, which in some cases can be beneficial. A non-VAT registered business only has to pay corporation tax, the rate of which varies but on the whole is lower than that of income tax.

On top of this, you can enjoy a greater level of copyright protection. Once a company name is registered with Companies House (the official database of all UK businesses), it can't be used again, so your brand is safer.

As you would expect, setting up this type of business is a more detailed process than becoming a sole trader, but it is far from onerous. The UK has one of the lightest regulatory regimes in the world and this is typified by the time and money it takes to set up a firm, neither of which is significant.

Once you have a business name and you know how many directors are involved (it could be just yourself), you can incorporate your business on the Companies House website for an admin fee of just £15.

Alternatively, you could go through a company formations platform (search online for names) that will register your business and combine this service with some essential business offers, like creating a basic website and designing business cards. These offers vary according to your budget and the service you choose, so scout around.

A third option is going through an accountancy company, some of which offer incorporation services as part of their introductory offer. You will probably need to sign up to a contract of 12 months or longer; it's up to your own calculations whether this is worth it or not.

All pretty straightforward so far, but becoming a limited business has its drawbacks too. The first is added paperwork. Directors have a duty to report on the business several times a year, in the form of an annual return and accounts, as well as yearly corporation tax statements and quarterly VAT statements if they are registered.

This adds up to more time working on the machinery of the business, which obviously robs precious hours winning contracts and completing projects. It's possible to mitigate this impact by outsourcing tax handling to an accountant, but this comes at a cost (see chapter 7).

Another key difference between sole traders and limited businesses is transparency. A sole trader can keep his or her earnings secret and doesn't have to declare anything publicly. Information about limited companies is public record, however. Anyone can find out who the shareholders are and how much of the business they own; they can access sales figures and other potentially sensitive bits of financial information.

You must be prepared, then, for new customers to access this information and use it in their decision to commission you or go with someone else.

# PARTNERSHIP

By far the least popular business structure of the three basic options is called a partnership. This combines elements of sole tradership and limited business. The business structure allows for multiple founders, but without some of the legal and tax obligations.

In some ways a partnership is the best of both worlds. Popular in the law and accountancy professions, it blends the simplicity and flexibility of sole trader status with the potential for growth of an incorporated business.

In a partnership, the founders are all self-employed. They come together to run the business, but they are personally and equally liable for all debts and legal action. Each partner must register with HMRC as self-employed and usually signs a partnership agreement with the other founders. Confusingly, a limited company can be one of the partners.

Partners manage the business and can recruit staff in the normal way. They can raise finance, for example a bank loan, but this must be secured against personal assets. All partners must complete annual returns as well as a group return for the partnership as a whole.

Any profits are distributed between the partners equally and those profits are subject to income tax and national insurance contributions.

A partnership is a less formal business structure than a limited business, but potentially more professional than sole trader status on its own. It's easy to get started and, as long as everyone is pulling in the same direction, it allows for fast and uncomplicated growth.

Working as a 'team of freelancers' means sharing the burden of business equally (owner managers often cite loneliness as a top downside to running a business) and you'll benefit from shared knowledge, experience, contacts and skills.

A partnership is also a closed loop, meaning you don't have to publish financial information or details of ownership, which is good news for those who value privacy.

But, as you might expect, there are negatives as well as positives. The first, shared with sole trader status, is that partners have liability for the business. This liability is shared (so in theory the more partners there are, the less exposure to each individual), but each individual must shoulder some of the risk.

As with sole traders, this liability has no limit and in extreme circumstances partners could find personal savings, assets and even their homes at risk of being seized by debtors' legal teams.

Public perceptions of partnerships vary. Their association with law and accountancy firms lends them weight, but the lack of reporting transparency might convince some potential customers to look elsewhere. A partnership is a fragile structure, dependent on all parties rowing together. Disagreements can be seriously damaging and, again, customers could be sensitive to this weakness in the company structure.

Lastly, there is the old adage that a camel is a horse made by a committee. Although partnerships benefit from shared knowledge and experience, it's possible they can be hamstrung by the requirement of all directors to agree. This can lead to outcomes that are diluted by compromise and, in extreme cases, inability to fulfil contracts.

# WHICH STRUCTURE IS RIGHT FOR YOU?

The business structure you choose is a personal choice influenced by many different factors. Usually these are fairly clear (for example, if you want to go into business with a friend then you can't be a sole trader without being in a partnership), so in most cases one format or other will jump out at you.

In very simple terms, sole trader status is good for people who want to stay small (although still potentially earn good money) and be free of complications from tax and red tape. Limited companies are for people who want to professionalise their business and factor in easy scope to grow. Partnerships are for those who want a bit of both and who share a vision for the future with a close friend or associate.

# BUSINESS LAW

*"I am always very conscientious about health and safety for myself and others. I have a lot of subcontractors that help with my bathrooms, including tiling and plastering. I always make sure everyone's insurance and equipment is correct and up to date."*

**– Simon Baker, Simon Baker Plumbing & Heating Ltd**

A company structure is a fundamental bedrock of the law as it affects business. But it's just the tip of the iceberg when it comes to the rules and regulations that influence how UK companies function, interact with each other and grow.

Running a business is a major responsibility, especially one that deals with the public regularly. There is also a major duty of care owed by company directors to staff members, who must be paid properly, cared for and managed sympathetically without overstepping the mark.

Business law changes every year in a process that tends to add new clauses and protections. In the last few years major new laws covering data protection (GDPR) and pensions (automatic enrolment) have fundamentally changed the way businesses operate in these fields.

There will be plenty more updates in future impacting areas of business as diverse as pay, harassment, contracts, information, equal opportunities, health and safety, property, copyright, libel and many more besides. Because the law changes constantly, it's a bad idea to try and cover it comprehensively in a book, but there are nevertheless some key areas that business owners should be aware of.

## Health and safety

For tradespeople, health and safety is one of the most relevant areas of law, much more so than in the case of industries where people work at desks (although these have to comply with stringent rules too). Trades men and women are mobile, they work with tools, often at height and in bad weather.

This increases the level of risk to business owners and their staff. In response, the authorities have sought to reduce the risk of injury and death in work accidents across the sector.

It's important work: research of 100,000 businesses conducted by insurance broker Simply Business found that tree surgery was the most dangerous trade in the UK, followed by roof tiling and scaffolding. Builders, landscape gardeners, plasterers and electricians all made the top ten.

Meanwhile, IronmongeryDirect, a supplier of ironmongery products, conducted research revealing that one in five tradespeople has had an accident at work, 70% of whom ended up in hospital (A&E) as a result.

The research also revealed that while 91% of tradespeople think health and safety courses are important, one in six have never attended a course and a whopping 41% don't use safety equipment. Meanwhile, a third admitted they weren't insured – more on that later in this chapter.

The Health and Safety at Work Act, signed in 1974, compels employers to look after the wellbeing of staff members. In essence this means taking all reasonable steps to identify obvious risks and counteract them with training, standard practices and safety equipment.

This means different things to different trades and while a hard hat and sturdy footwear is absolutely essential on a building site, thick gloves and eye protection are the go-to safety accessories when it comes to tree surgery. Safety harnesses and high visibility vests are relevant to both in different scenarios.

> "It's incredibly difficult for small businesses and start-ups with no funds to use on this sort of thing. I was fortunate to come from a background of plumbing where I worked my way up into management so had a good understanding of most areas.
>
> "We invested in health and safety kit for employees such as gloves, knee pads, goggles, ear defenders and first aid boxes, but also all the other things such as insurance. The list is endless.
>
> "We discovered the Federation of Small Businesses (FSB) and its annual fee is nothing compared to the benefits of every legal document you could possibly think of being ready to download and modify to suit your business. It is a no brainer if you are ready to expand as it takes all that worry, pressure and cost away."

*– Jordan Williams, JR Williams Plumbing Services Ltd*

> "Health and safety is very important. I use a third-party system to produce risk assessments and method statements, which is not only sensible to ensure you are considering or mitigating all risks, but also helps you secure some of the bigger contractors.
>
> "Mr and Mrs Jones won't want to see all the paperwork, they just need to know that you work safely and are covered by relevant insurance should things go wrong, but Jones Incorporated will be more than impressed if you provide a full risk assessment and method statement pack with your tenders on the larger projects. We have the systems to do this quickly."

*– Chris Fairbairn, Cribbit Installations Ltd*

Companies must carry out and document a risk assessment under the guidelines of the Health and Safety Executive and prove that they have met the resulting obligations. Failure to do so could result in serious penalties, especially if negligence results in injury to an employee or member of the public.

# SUCCESS STORIES ||||➡

**Name:** Chris Fairbairn
**Business name:** Cribbit Installations
**Type of business:** Kitchen, bedroom and bathroom supply and installation
**Number of employees:** 1

### How did you get started in your trade?

"After buying a house to renovate and sell on, I decided to leave the security of a job in DIY retail management to become a tradesman. Initially I completed an electrical course and became an NICEIC-approved domestic installer."

### Has the business changed since you started?

"After watching and learning from other trades while completing electrical work for them, I moved into kitchen and bathroom fitting. Since then I have expanded the business to where it is now – manufacturing our own range of kitchens and fitted bedrooms, retailing bathroom products and flooring, with teams of fitters installing for me."

### Describe your typical customer and project.

"Our typical customer is a homeowner looking to improve their property. With kitchens and bathrooms being such fundamental rooms, these are often the larger projects people don't want to take on themselves. They also don't usually want to arrange each trade themselves, so being experts in product and installation we can now take care of it all with one quote to supply and fit and transform these fundamental rooms."

### What do you enjoy about your career?

"I love creating a design to match what the customer is looking for, then manufacturing and sourcing product and overseeing installations to create the new rooms. There is a real sense of achievement looking at a quality finished room, knowing that I'm helping to support the fitters in their work."

### What's the hardest thing about it, or the biggest challenge you face?

"Time and work-life balance are the biggest challenges by far. There is so much more I could be doing, that I want to be doing to drive the business forward. But I'm just one person and sometimes I like to go home too. The phone is always on, work is always there."

### What are your plans for the future?

"To market the business better, showcase my own products and services, ultimately leading more confirmed projects to keep the fitters busy. Then hopefully reaching a point where I can employ help and the business can stretch its legs."

### What's your best tip for other tradespeople in your sector?

"Find what you are good at, concentrate on doing that and do it well. There's no point working hard to create quality work and then keeping quiet about it. Customer service is key too; keep people informed, give them a great customer journey. They will then tell their story and generate more leads, which is where Checkatrade fits in to help support that process."

# EMPLOYMENT LAW

Employment law is a vast, sprawling set of regulations governing the way employers and their staff work together. It sets a base-level standard for the treatment of workers and sets out the circumstances under which people can be disciplined, made redundant or fired.

A fine balance is needed to give adequate protections to individuals while also allowing businesses the freedom to make money and grow, so it's no surprise that employment law is subject to regular revisions. What follows is the basic areas you must focus on as an employer.

## *The recruitment process*

If you interview candidates for a job then your final decision to hire must be based on the individual's credentials and how they fit the requirements of the role. You can't discriminate on the basis of age, gender, race or disability unless you can give a clear and obvious reason for doing so (only men can apply for jobs as male models, for example).

Candidates, including those who don't get a job, can request to view any notes relevant to their application. It's important, therefore, to document the reasons they weren't hired and to keep this evidence safe.

As covered in chapter 6, you must provide written terms and conditions to your new employee. This should include the terms of work, holiday, hours and in general what is expected of them. But an employee is protected by basic employment laws as soon as they accept a job offer, regardless of whether it's verbal or in writing.

Once agreed and signed, a written contract cannot be changed without consent of both employer and employee.

## *Working conditions, pay and holidays*

The UK has a number of hard-and-fast rules that employers can't ignore. For example, workers can't be forced to work more than 48 hours a week and you have to consider flexible working requests from people who've worked for you more than 26 weeks.

Part-timers have the same rights as full-time employees and everyone has the right to parental leave when they have children. They must be paid at least the national minimum wage, around £8 an hour for people over the age of 25, and employers are responsible for deducting the right level of income tax and national insurance from wages.

If a worker falls ill or is injured, you must cover their time off for up to 28 weeks at a statutory rate of currently just under £100 per week.

## Rights and protections

Much of this is common sense, but employees have rights that prevent exploitation and ill-treatment. They should be free to join a trade union and after a month's work are entitled to a notice period if made redundant.

The working relationship has to be undertaken with due care and trust – this cuts both ways – and you can't infringe a worker's right to a private life. Perhaps most importantly, you can't discriminate on the basis of gender, race, age, disability or religious beliefs.

If you employ people with disabilities, you must take 'reasonable' measures to ensure they can do the job effectively. In essence, that means removing any obvious barriers that impede work. The word 'reasonable' protects employers from having to spend large sums or undertake major work that would harm the business's normal operations.

When it comes to disciplinary proceedings, redundancy or firing, there is a straightforward code of practice. Essentially, this means making it clear what actions or offences would activate disciplinary proceedings and keeping employees informed of any action against them verbally and in writing.

## Legal representation and insurance

As mentioned, business law is a big and complicated subject to get on top of. Employing the services of a law firm and getting adequately insured are therefore two essential steps. A legal service can ensure you tick all the boxes and provide you with all the necessary documents to operate and employ people, while insurance will protect you from the downside of unexpected events.

The best advice is to seek expert opinion on necessary measures. Search online for 'business law help' and 'insurance for tradespeople' for information on how to move forward.

# WHERE AND HOW TO FIND A LAWYER?

Lawyers are a bit like tradespeople: when you find a good one you should hang on to them. But how do you get a cost-effective solicitor who can cover your needs? The Law Society is a great first step; the organisation offers a searchable database of nearly 170,000 legal specialists and you can browse by location and expertise, be it dispute resolution, regulation and compliance or intellectual property. Visit **www.lawsociety.org.uk** and, on the homepage, click the tab marked 'Find a solicitor'.

# CHAPTER NINE

*Nailing Strategy and Planning Expansion*

"If you want to hit the big time it's important to keep one eye on a brighter future."

**B**ig ideas fuel business growth, so if you want to hit the big time it's important to keep one eye on a brighter future while you're dealing with the machinations of the present. As a busy person juggling multiple customers, systems and processes, this can be a tricky balancing act, but creating a growth plan could save you hours of wasted effort down the track.

> "Work on retaining existing customers. Three quarters of our work pool is from existing customers. They get you through recessions and help you to stay busy throughout the year. It's important to retain customers, if you start off by retaining customers then you won't go wrong."

*– Charlie Mullins, Pimlico Plumbers*

If you have followed the advice laid out in chapter 4, then you should have a clear vision for progress and understand the broad steps that will take you there. This strategy should read like an ambitious business plan, incorporating all of the opportunities out there, as well as the things that could trip you up.

Now comes the thorny task of actually achieving your goals. Strategies are useless if, once written, they are parked on a shelf. Use your plan like you might do a map; check it regularly to remind you of your ambitions and prevent your business from steering off course.

> "We are always looking for opportunities within the industry. For example, we'll take on small carpentry jobs and look for property we can refurbish ourselves. We have also looked into buying and managing freehold buildings within the company. We are keen to take on larger projects in the future and have become VAT-registered in order to become more attractive to the commercial market. We are a limited company, which I feel is important and looks professional."

*– Chris Jones, LSW Decorating Ltd*

# ROUTES TO GROWTH

Regardless of whether you paint walls, clean houses or put up fences for a living, the broad opportunities to grow your business are the same. The two most obvious are to attract new customers and to sell more to existing ones – and we've covered these topics in chapter 4. But there are less well-trodden routes to growth that can have dramatic results too.

## *Diversify into new markets*

A lot of successful businesses start out doing one thing and end up doing another. This is because the owner or a member of staff spots an opportunity in a related field where there's better scope to earn revenue and grow.

Tradespeople are not excluded from this opportunity and there are several ways in which businesses in this sector change tack or expand into new markets. One is simply bolting on additional services as you grow; this gives a business a 'full-service' edge, allowing people to book your team to work on bigger, more complicated projects.

> "We are a home-improvement business and are experts in windows, doors, driveways and conservatories. We have invested in new staff and added kitchens and bathrooms as our newest products.
>
> "In the last year my business partner and I have invested every penny we have made back into the business which has helped us grow to a level where we now have two offices and a storage unit. We have the equivalent of more than 50 staff, commissioning self-employed people as well as in-house staff and CIS-registered fitters."

– **Alan Gough, Warmglow Home Improvements Ltd**

Another common method is creating a product that helps you deliver your service. It could be better paint, a new style of brush, sheers that cut more effectively or a gadget that makes wiring a wall more straightforward. They say necessity is the mother of invention; tradespeople are well placed to understand a need and to create something which satisfies it.

A third way to diversify is to expand territorially. Extending your reach opens you up to more customers and gives you a bigger pond in which to fish for big projects. This is a great opportunity if you know your offer outclasses rivals in a nearby postcode.

## Subcontract

Subcontracting works both ways. If you are good at winning business then you can be ambitious, broadening your sales attack and engaging trusted partners to help you fulfil the work. Subcontracting is a brilliant way to grow while you create the necessary funds to start recruiting more full-time workers.

On the flip-side, if the quality of your work is brilliant and you are naturally better at fulfilling projects than pitching for them, you might consider subcontracting for others. Making friends in similar trades will vastly increase your pipeline of potential jobs.

## Mergers and acquisitions

Mergers and acquisitions might sound like something for large companies, but buying another business is a legitimate growth tactic for any business. It might be that a rival is retiring, or that a business that complements your own is winning contracts that you could work on too.

Whatever the case, merging with a business or acquiring it should give you an economy of scale with better profit margins. You'll get all of the branding, equipment and the workforce, which could deliver your business into the big time.

You'll probably need to borrow money for a major investment like this, but sources of funding are always looking for ambitious companies with realistic expansion plans. If you can demonstrate a big upside to your acquisition or merger, you could find yourself spoilt for choice. More on raising money later in this chapter.

Whichever way you choose to grow your business, be prepared to change your mindset, as well as your style of management. Running a one-man band requires a very different skillset to presiding over multiple projects and a diverse workforce.

"We grew from a husband-and-wife start-up into a small business, thriving in our local community. A huge part of this story involves the sourcing of like-minded engineers, with similar values to us. We very much felt that the company was our baby and that people working under our name reflected on us directly.

"We live in a small community where reputation is everything. But finding the right engineer to join our team was only the start, we had to familiarise ourselves with the role of employer and take on board its responsibilities.

"We have had to become motivational, inspirational and responsible. Sometimes there have been great leaps of faith and sometimes decisions have happened after deep discussion. But seven years later, with the help of Checkatrade, we have built something we are very proud of."

**– Louise Kirk, RH Heating and Plumbing Ltd**

# SUCCESS STORIES ⫟⫟⫟⫟⬤➤

**Name:** Louise Kirk
**Business name:** RH Heating and Plumbing
**Type of business:** Heating and plumbing services
**Number of employees:** 4

### How did you get started in your trade?

"My husband worked in the heating industry all his life, but wanted to venture out on his own. In the beginning, it was just him; I organised a bit of paperwork alongside other work.

"We were desperate for the phone to ring. Even if you're a good engineer it doesn't equate to being a good business person. We gave each customer the best service we could and hoped that at the end of the year the figures would add up."

### Has the business changed since you started?

"Within months our biggest problem was meeting demand, even with my husband working seven days a week, so we took on an apprentice. It was a step up for me as an employer with new responsibilities I had to get my head around. We incorporated the business and have continued to grow from there.

"I am now based in the office full-time. My role varies from collecting parts to payroll and booking work. I think the customers appreciate the personal touch. As the first point of contact, I usually know their name or property address."

### Describe your typical customer and project.

"What I love about our role in the community is the variety of jobs and customers. We work for private householders, landlords, estate agents and charities with local public buildings. Some of our projects are complete rebuilds, over months, coordinating with other trades; others are one-offs to replace some tap washers."

### What do you enjoy about your career?

"I like all the roles I play, but for me the most rewarding part of the job is when a customer has been over-quoted for work from other tradesmen and then receives our carefully calculated estimate."

### What's the hardest thing about it, or the biggest challenge you face?

"One of the biggest challenges we face is the bad reputations of other tradespeople. Our first contact is often with a customer let down by another company. In this case we start on the back foot as they think all plumbers will be late, overcharge or not turn up.

"I see it as a personal challenge to turn that perception around; seeing the feedback our customers leave on the Checkatrade website is always a boost."

### What are your plans for the future?

"We are constantly weighing up if we should expand or not, there are benefits and drawbacks for each direction. So far we have let the company evolve itself."

### What's your best tip for other tradespeople in your sector?

"My top tip is to be kind. Even after seven years, I still look at every job

from the customer's point of view: would I feel it offers value for money? Is the work disruptive to a household? Is the estimate clear? Do I understand the work involved?

"What keeps us going is the huge sense of satisfaction knowing that we couldn't have done anything better."

# PLANNING FOR GROWTH

Without direction, growth can do more harm than good. Over the years an uncountable number of businesses have overextended themselves, causing them to run out of cash, deliver poor quality or become stretched in terms of personnel – sometimes all three at the same time.

In this case a business can find itself worse off than before, having lost valued staff to fatigue as well as cherished customers fed up with the drop in quality. At worst it can spell the end of the business – so planning is a must.

"Always have a goal: where you want to be, how big you want the company to get. After that you need to consider how to do it."

**– Matt Merry, Matt Merry Roofing**

The first question to ask is 'why do we want to grow?' and 'what objective do we want to fulfil?'. It could be scaling up for acquisition by a rival, or more simply stretching out profit margins and picking up lots of new work. Different goals require different paths to growth and these will give you a good idea of what you need to get where you're going.

Next, referring to your sales strategy, answer the following questions:

- Who is our ideal customer?
- What is our competitive advantage?
- Where are the spaces in what we do well?

- What are the most obvious areas for growth?
- Can we create new revenue streams – if so which ones?
- Can we develop partnerships to fuel growth?
- Are there any blind corners or red herrings we should avoid?

This exercise should take a couple of hours, but its value is in guiding the business towards the things that deliver revenue and profit, and away from those that take up time and energy without the sort of benefits that make it worthwhile.

> "We now cover three locations and have expanded the area we work in. We've made some off-the-cuff decisions for expansion that have been costly and expensive, including taking on staff at short notice and not having enough people to cover the whole of our area.
>
> "It's so, so important to plan for growth and have milestones by which you can check your growth trajectory. Sometimes it looks like you're doing well but if you're not meeting the tests you set out at the beginning of the process you have to really think about whether it's working."

*– Adam Allsop, The Shutter Studio Ltd*

> "We had a strategy from day one with the simple guideline 'don't grow too big too quick'. With this industry, it only takes a couple of large jobs on the books and the financial outlay is massive before you get a return."

*– Jordan Williams, JR Williams Plumbing Services Ltd*

# MENTORS

There's nothing new under the sun, or so they say. In other words, unless your plans are completely outlandish then people will have gone through the same or similar experiences in the past. These experiences will have imbued them with firsthand knowledge of the good, bad and ugly of business growth.

People who have been successful in business probably have experience of customers, sales, marketing, finance and team-building – all in the context of a changing (expanding) business environment. It's information you can't buy.

This, in essence, is the value of a mentor. They can steer you away from bad decisions and towards the kind of actions they know have worked in the past. A good mentor could help you win major contracts, or just as easily save you money by advising against a poor investment.

> "If you're a painter and decorator like me, look for the best decorator working around you. They might be a tradesperson on a local site or a lecturer at your college. Stick with them. Working with someone who's a master of their trade, you'll pick up information and tips that could take years to develop.
>
> "It always good to learn from everyone around you and pool all of the knowledge together. These snippets of information are ingredients of the recipe that will build your business."

**– Wayne de Wet, Wayne de Wet Painting and Decorating Services**

Many tradespeople are – or have been – part of a family business, usually composed of a parent and one or more children. The younger generation learns from the older one and the business develops naturally over time.

Other people pick up mentors via events and trade shows, often because they hit it off with someone during a conversation. Still more are connected with mentors through official programmes and networking events laid on by business groups and other institutions.

If you don't have access to these routes, it might be a good idea to go direct and get in touch with someone you know by reputation and who you respect – perhaps someone you would like to emulate.

A quick email takes no time at all and it just might be the start of a fruitful business relationship. The worst that can happen is that your target mentor doesn't respond – which is hardly the end of the world. Try something like this:

*Dear* _____

*My name's ABC and I run a small business as an XYZ. I have watched your business's progress over the years and I think you've done a brilliant job. I wondered if I could ask your advice on a couple of matters to do with growing my own business. I'm ambitious and eager to learn, maybe I could buy you a cup of coffee one day soon?*

*All the best,* _____

If you catch someone in the right mood, this approach really does work. Most people are happy to give up a small amount of time to help others and some actively relish the prospect of helping others grow, maybe as part of a commitment to 'give something back'.

It might work, it might not, but the potential benefits far outweigh the time and effort it takes to make an approach like the one above.

# RAISING MONEY

Business owners seek funding for a range of reasons. In chapter 5, we looked at borrowing to buy a van and businesses also borrow to bridge gaps in cash flow. A third reason is to invest in growth by investing in more (or better) equipment, taking on staff, moving to bigger premises or ploughing funds into sales and marketing.

This kind of activity is probably the most attractive to financial firms and to wider sources of funding such as business angels (private individuals with spare cash to invest in businesses) and venture capital firms (professional businesses set up to invest money in promising firms in the hope their stake will grow).

If you're planning something very ambitious and you need a lot of money, you need to demonstrate why investors should trust you with their cash. In most cases you will submit a business plan (a variation of your sales strategy) with an emphasis on proving that your investment will either allow you to pay the money back with interest (in the case of a loan) or that your business will grow and return an inflated sum to your backer (in the case of a business angel or venture capitalist).

Banks, venture capital and crowdfunding platforms will ask for a lot of evidence to back up your claims and in many cases they will perform 'due diligence', which essentially means forensically checking the facts to ensure what you say is true.

In most cases, this takes a lot of preparation, time and effort – even money – and it can upset the normal running of the business by distracting the top managers for long periods, so it's not for the faint-hearted. It's important to give it plenty of consideration because a failed bid for funding can set a business back.

# RISK VERSUS REWARD

Growth is a risky business, but sometimes you just have to go for it. If you are entrepreneurial and are in business to develop your company into a major player, you'll need to identify every opportunity that comes your way and grab it with both hands.

Sometimes the timing won't suit you. In that case, having good judgement is a real asset. Is it better to jump at the chance to grow and risk the consequences or stay conservative and stick to a well thought-out plan? Only you can decide.

"The next stage always comes up quicker than you expect. Here I am sat in an industrial unit twice the size of my old one, because it became available in a good location at a good price, not because I was ready for it.

"I am now planning to make more space and start manufacturing our own products – again, not because I was ready, but because the opportunity presented itself and if I didn't do it now I would miss it. This needs a lot of logistical and financial planning to make it happen, as well as a robust marketing plan to ensure the enquiries keep ramping up to cover the extra work needed.

"The company structure will need to be addressed, as will getting the right people in place, new systems, new health and safety planning. Most importantly, more sales to support all this. Growing a business isn't easy, but with the right support around you and the right mindset, you can do it."

**– Chris Fairbairn, Cribbit Installations Ltd**

# CHAPTER TEN

*How HomeServe
Accelerated*

"The early part of the HomeServe story was all about getting established, finding partners, creating products, accelerating fast and building an enormous base of happy customers."

# FROM ZERO TO 1 MILLION CUSTOMERS

When it first opened for business HomeServe employed only 20 people in a corner of the South Staffordshire Water Company building in Walsall. Twenty-five years later, the HomeServe group employs more than 3,000 staff in the UK alone, operates locations across North America and Europe, and boasts a market capitalisation of over £3bn.

HomeServe provides 8.4m customers with a service that frees them from the worry and inconvenience of home emergencies and repairs. Its major international businesses in North America, France and Spain contribute over half of the group's operating profit. HomeServe companies have access to 109m affinity partner households worldwide and the famous red vans are a familiar sight in communities from Massachusetts to Madrid.

So how did a small subsidiary of a British water utility grow into a global force in the support services sector?

## STARTING OUT

The HomeServe story begins in 1993. Richard Harpin and Jeremy Middleton first met in the marketing department of the influential consumer goods company Procter and Gamble. The two established a strong friendship and realised they had similar career goals. Over the next few years they set up a number of businesses, starting with property management and then moving into service-based companies offering, among other things, decorating and ironing.

They also set up a home emergency repair service called FastFix. FastFix was the forerunner of HomeServe, with operatives answering call-outs for all kinds of domestic emergencies. Richard and Jeremy were experienced marketeers and knew how to craft a message and deliver it to the right people, so demand was high.

But there was a fly in the ointment: they couldn't find a cost-effective way to supply a service to meet demand. They didn't have enough experience in running a network of contractors and in one year the business lost £100,000.

At that point, many people would give up. They were forced to use credit cards to get the company through cash flow problems and reached an agreement with the tax office to postpone payment of the company's bill. Perhaps this was the moment to quit and cut their losses?

# A NEW APPROACH

There was one more avenue to explore. Richard noticed that most emergency calls were for plumbers and he started to think about the potential synergy between service companies like FastFix and large utility companies. He had seen the way British Gas marketed their boiler breakdown service and wondered if a joint venture between FastFix and a water company might be the solution to their problems.

The UK's water utility sector had recently gone through a programme of privatisation, which meant that British water companies were on the lookout for new business opportunities. Jeremy approached all the water utilities with a proposal to provide consultancy advice on starting up a plumbing service. Only one of them agreed to meet up – South Staffordshire Water Holdings.

Jeremy pitched the idea and they commissioned a consultancy review to explore the proposal. Richard drove down the motorway to the West Midlands for an eight week contract to work on the review... and he never left.

South Staffs was already considering setting up a regional plumbing business. Richard and Jeremy concluded this was the wrong way to go. Instead, they proposed a national emergency plumbing service run as a franchise operation.

The review identified two potential challenges: South Staffs didn't have managers with entrepreneurial skills to set up a new business and, ideally, they needed to acquire a small, emergency repairs service company to test the idea. Fortunately, Richard and Jeremy had solutions to those problems: South Staffs could set up a joint venture with FastFix and Richard would run it for them.

# A SUPPORTIVE SHAREHOLDER

Did South Staffs get a good deal? The board invested £100,000 to set up the new business and negotiated a 52/48 division of shares in their favour. The business plan projected a £1m profit by year five, but that target proved to be wildly inaccurate. The business made closer to £7m profit. It was a very good deal for South Staffs, particularly as it included an option for them to increase their stake to 75%, which they exercised at the first opportunity.

The board members of South Staffs were a good judge of character. They invested in the business and put their faith in Richard's entrepreneurial skills. In return, the parent company ended up owning the lion's share of the business, creating substantial profits for its shareholders. But Jeremy didn't lose any sleep over that:

> "South Staffs were a very supportive shareholder. Yes, we would have liked to have held on to more of the company, but it was a fair deal. Let's just say the most important thing is to grow the cake and not to worry too much about how it's cut."

Having come up with the idea for an emergency plumbing service, it was Richard who had to make it work. He remembers the glamour of his first workstation:

"By the end of the year we had 20 people, including a few people to answer the phones, someone to do the finances, and a secretary. We took a very little space on the ground floor of the water company building, behind the reception. I think previously it had been their post room."

The team worked hard in that first year. Once again, the marketing was good and with South Staffs providing administrative support Richard was able to run a professional sales and customer service. At this stage FastFix was working on a simple pay-per-job basis and the marketing was done through classified ads in the *Yellow Pages*.

# CHALLENGES

The challenges were on the operations side. To meet demand Richard had to recruit quickly and the company over-promised on what it could deliver for franchisees. Service standards were lower than he wanted and the pay-per-job model still didn't make a profit. Richard learned a valuable lesson: if a small business isn't making money, growing it into a bigger business won't magically transform the bottom line.

The losses multiplied and by the end of the first year FastFix had lost half a million pounds. With hindsight that was not a significant loss for South Staffs, although at the time Richard was concerned they might close the company down. His friends and business colleagues were telling him he should start looking for a salaried job. This was a personal challenge and a turning point in the HomeServe story.

"I saw the HomeServe business as the last throw of the dice. If I couldn't make it work then I'd have to be content with employment rather than self-employment. I think one of the things I've learnt so far in life is if you really believe in something and stick with it, there is always light at the end of the tunnel... It won't happen in the way that you originally planned, but it's about being nimble and flexible and finding a way of making it work."

# A NEW MODEL

Richard had to find a model delivering the service customers wanted, at a price that would generate a profit. Revenues from the pay-per-job model were unpredictable and when there was a lull in call-outs, the company still had to cover business costs.

What he needed was a guaranteed income stream. Richard had come across a small water company in southern England running a plumbing insurance service that seemed quite successful. He decided to investigate and hired a market research company to carry out focus groups with the water company's customers.

> "I remember sitting in a room in a Holiday Inn in Surrey, listening to their customers talking about what they liked about the service and what they didn't like. So we took all the things they liked... and then with the things they didn't like, we just took them out of the product. I also had some ideas on what we should add in, and that was the basis of us setting up our Home Service plan."

Richard listened to the focus groups and heard customers were concerned about their responsibility for the pipes running from the house to the mains supply. The connecting pipes often ran under walls, lawns, or driveways, and they didn't feel confident about finding someone qualified to come out in an emergency to repair a leak. He decided to make this the cornerstone of the new insurance product. For an annual subscription of £39, members were guaranteed a 24-hour emergency repair service for their underground water supply pipe, up to a total cost of £500. Membership also gave them similar cover on drains and sewers, as well as cover up to a maximum of £150 for any internal plumbing emergency work.

This new membership service was an insurance product, so before they could sell it Richard needed an insurance company to underwrite the policies. The underwriter takes a set fee and agrees to cover the cost of any claim on the policy. But plumbing insurance was a relatively new product, which meant insurers didn't have enough data from previous years to accurately calculate the level of risk.

Richard's solution was simple – he told them what he could afford to pay them out of the customer's annual premium and asked if that was enough to cover the insurance risk. One company, AXA Assistance, took it on, and HomeServe is still working with them today.

# TAKING THE IDEA TO MARKET

The next step was to test the market. The first direct mail leaflet explained in simple terms the homeowner's responsibility for the water supply pipe running from the water main in the road to the home, then laid out the HomeServe cover. On the front was a cartoon of a couple standing on their lawn and watching helplessly as a fountain of water erupts through manicured grass. The company sent out a thousand leaflets to customers in the South Staffordshire area, hoping for something approaching the 1% take up considered respectable for direct mail campaigns.

There was a 3.8% take up, which in the business of direct mail marketing is a resounding success. With 1,000 leaflets mailed out, 38 people responded and took out a £39 annual subscription, bringing in a total of £1,482.

That, at a basic level, is how you start a £3bn business. Richard knew it couldn't be a fluke. Over the years, HomeServe tried out a range of home insurance products and a number of different marketing strategies in the UK and internationally. As you would expect, the company has seen different take ups for those campaigns. Sometimes it's less than the 3.8% they achieved with that first mailshot, sometimes more.

Richard's other key insight in those early days was his appreciation of the role played by HomeServe's affinity partners. The success of the marketing wasn't only down to the new service, it was also the importance of the South Staffordshire Water brand on the leaflet.

People trusted their water company to provide them with a reliable emergency plumbing service.

Richard didn't rest on his laurels. He realised that what worked with South Staffordshire Water was going to work with every other water utility company in the UK – and now he didn't have to offer 52% of the business, just a commission.

> "Once the idea was proved with South Staffs, I went to Anglian Water and got them to agree a marketing plan to do exactly what we were doing for South Staffs, but paying them a commission to use their name. That was the magic business model. After Anglian, we went out and signed most of the UK water companies."

By the end of the 1997/98 financial year, HomeServe had half a million members, doubled turnover again to £14m, signed affinity partnerships with South East Water, Thames Water, Affinity Water (Central and South East), and Southern Water, and created operating profit of nearly £5m to the South Staffordshire Water accounts, which represented approximately 30% of the group's operating profit.

# NEW PRODUCTS

During this period, HomeServe experimented with new products. There were plans to create a policy combining plumbing, heating, electrics, and telecoms cover, as well as a bill-payment protection policy and a recovery service for keys and personal possessions, which used unique identity tags. Richard also decided to take on the giant British Gas, offering a rival central heating cover plan at a slightly lower cost. The marketing team was creating ten new ideas before breakfast; the trick was to work out which was right for the business.

And it produced another significant challenge. When the marketing and sales team are doubling demand year-on-year, the rest of the company has to keep pace. How do you ramp up to meet that demand? And how do you put in place quality control measures to maintain standards? It's a good problem to have, but a problem all the same.

Jennifer Synnott was director of customer services and at the heart of the HomeServe operation in those early years. She recalls what it was like keeping pace with Richard's determination to corner the market:

> "We'd go to one of the water companies and we'd end up with a new affinity partner – and once that was done, Richard was on to the next thing. Following behind was poor old me, trying to get the infrastructure in place with very little cash. Quite often we were having to persuade South Staffs to knock down some walls to make our space even bigger."

# CUSTOMER EXPERIENCE

The key to the success of the HomeServe business, then as now, was quality customer experience. Richard started FastFix because he had seen how hard it was to contact a reliable plumber in an emergency; HomeServe addressed the need. Reliability was also the cornerstone of the partnership model: the public trusted the affinity partner brands and HomeServe was responsible for repaying their trust.

HomeServe's operations team worked to improve the service, providing training and technical support to the network. They understood the importance of the role; operations remains the linchpin of the organisation.

The training wasn't focused exclusively on technical skills. HomeServe has always prided itself on the way its engineers approach a job and their attention to detail.

# SALES AND MARKETING

Every department makes an invaluable contribution to the success of the company, whether it's IT services, legal, customer services, accounts, design, social media – all of them play their role. But one department has probably contributed more than any other: sales and marketing.

As the business grew, the department developed an acquisition function, a customer marketing function, and a product function. Marketing became less focused on sectors and more concerned with stages in the customer's journey. A challenge with splitting up marketing into different teams is showing everyone they are part of a central strategy. The acquisition team's focus on bringing in new customers has to take into account the company's wider objective to retain customers for the long-term. New customers who join for the right reasons are also more likely to purchase other products from the customer marketing team.

# OUTGROWING THE POST ROOM

The core full-time team, which had quickly outgrown the old post room, initially moved onto the second floor of the South Staffs' building and then, finally, into a new office block built on the South Staffs car park. Jennifer Synnott remembers the first time she walked around the building with Richard and Brian Whitty, the chief executive of South Staffs:

> "I think Brian was getting the jitters because we had this huge great open space, and we'd only got around 50 staff at the time, all shoved in a tiny little area... Brian was saying, 'What if we don't fill it?' and Richard was saying, 'Of course we're going to fill it. We're going to fill it in two years.' We filled it in a year and we were on to the next thing."

When you talk to people who have worked at HomeServe it becomes clear that it is a company built on strong, supportive working relationships. The company culture is a virtuous circle: if someone helps you when you need it, you will help other people in turn.

This approach is carried over into one of the most important elements in the HomeServe business model, the relationship with affinity partners. From the first partnership with South Staffordshire Water to the initial market testing with Anglian Water, affinity partnerships have been at the heart of the business. In six years, HomeServe built a network of affinity partners that included most of the major British water companies and a range of other well-known brands, such as the gas boiler manufacturers Vaillant and Ideal.

HomeServe listens to its affinity partners and looks for ways to add value. It tries to go the extra mile, sharing ideas, systems and customer feedback with its partners. Those early affinity partner relationships were the foundation stones of the business.

By 1999 the business that Richard started six years before in the old post room, with nothing more than a desk and a phone, was now as big as the parent company. In July that year it was listed on the London Stock Exchange.

# FAST FORWARD TO TODAY

The early part of the HomeServe story was all about getting established, finding partners, creating products, accelerating fast and building an enormous base of happy customers. Since 2000, the focus has been on growth on a whole new level. The business has developed organically and through acquisitions to solidify its presence in domestic and international territories.

A highlight in the growth curve came in 2017, with the $143m purchase of the home repair services business of Dominion Products and Services from one of the largest utility companies in the US. The deal brought a large number of new partnerships, policies and partner relationships into the HomeServe family of businesses.

The same year HomeServe acquired Checkatrade, the thriving community of approved, recommended tradespeople, in two tranches. It also snapped up Checkatrade's Spanish equivalent, Habitissimo, to expand its presence in continental Europe. This expansion, which is also in evidence in more than a dozen major acquisitions since 2000, reflects the company's ambition and its refusal to stand still.

The results of all this speak for themselves. The latest preliminary results show operating profit up 29% to £135m; a 146% increase in profit and 20% customer uplift across North America; double-digit profit growth in France and Spain; and, of course, further scope to expand with Checkatrade evolving into an on-demand home experts marketplace.

This is a tribute to a company on the move and in many ways it's in sharp contrast to HomeServe's early years as FastFix, when the founders flew by the seat of their pants to create a business proposition that worked for both customers and their profit margins. However, while this corporate growth seems miles away from those early days, really it's all down to the same core principles that fuel great businesses: guts, ingenuity and a complete unwillingness to let setbacks get in the way of a great idea.

## Get support from Enterprise Nation

❝ If you're reading this and are starting or growing a trades business, you know it comes with a tough job description. You have to perfect your service, manage money, attract customers – and keep those customers coming back. Hard work, it may be. Gratifying, most definitely.

I founded Enterprise Nation in 2005, to create a more entrepreneurial society in the UK and help people start, run and grow a successful business. Since then we've supported more than 70,000 small businesses to turn their good ideas into great businesses.

When people ask me the favourite bit of my job, it's easy to reply. It is hearing from our small business members on their successes; hearing how they've turned their business idea into a reality and founded on the back of the daily support we deliver.

In more than ten years of providing enterprise support, we've seen that businesses that access support grow faster than those that don't. Support from your peers who are happy to share what worked for them, and support from experts and advisers who have spent years perfecting their practice so you don't have to. With Enterprise Nation membership, that support is just a click away! 🙶

**Emma Jones**
*Founder, Enterprise Nation*

Make the most of the opportunities to grow your trades business by joining today: **enterprisenation.com/ membership**

*What's in it for your trades business?*

## Find answers

Access all the resources you need in just a couple of clicks, attend weekly online masterclasses and explore recommendations to grow your business.

## Personalised support

Seeking help and advice is often the key to success! With an adviser search, easily compare services available and get tailored support from the expert community.

## Grow your network

Meet journalists, funders and potential customers to give a real boost to your business and create valuable connections with fellow business owners.

## Save money

Access a range of exclusive discounts including 25% off all Enterprise Nation events, free networking meet-ups and deals on business essentials such as business cards and insurance.

# CHAPTER ELEVEN

*The Checkatrade*
*Story*

"For Kevin, making money is best when it happens as a by-product of doing some good. He has spent 20 years eliminating businesses who think differently."

A tornado is a rare event in Selsey, a sleepy seaside town on West Sussex's southern tip. But one night in January 1998, a 100mph wind funnel powered its way inland, ripping off roofs, uprooting trees and in one case collapsing the entire exterior wall of a home.

The house's occupant, Jeremy Wearn, was awoken by the crashing sound of the room around him being torn apart. He hid under his duvet and waited in terror for the storm to pass. When he emerged, the bedroom had three sides instead of the customary four. Interviewed later on TV news, he described the incident as "horrendous... it was so noisy, so bad".

Juicy stories like his, plus the estimated £10m worth of damage to property, made the Selsey Tornado a national sensation. Stories were churned out and media consumers gobbled them up; not least an army of tradespeople who sensed a business opportunity.

"Tradesmen from all over the UK flooded the area," remembers Kevin Byrne, a Selsey resident who, at the time, worked as a graphic designer. "The authorities acted – they stopped 175 white vans entering the town. They had bald tires, no MOT, no insurance or tax.

"But a lot got in and stories started to emerge of rogue traders preying on vulnerable members of the community. They would offer to help and then charge £1,000 to put up a tarpaulin, or £600 to replace a few roof tiles. People were being ripped off.

"It made me angry. If you shoplift a bottle of wine you'll get arrested and probably prosecuted. You could even get a custodial sentence. But in 1998 people could go into someone's home, take their money and leave the property a mess, and it seemed like no one could stop them."

The thought preyed on Kevin's mind. He says it wasn't a lightbulb moment exactly, but it gestated for a few months before he decided to act.

He made a few calls. Trading Standards told him about the process of catching up with rogue traders, but admitted there wasn't a good way to prevent individual cases of dishonesty before they happened. Various guilds and federations gave him roughly the same line. Shady dealers could ruin someone's day, take the money and disappear into  the sunset – and there was nothing anyone could do to stop them.

Seven years earlier Kevin had set up a small business distributing a business directory in the area. It was standard fare: size A5, colourful, lots of local advertising. But in light of what he'd learned, he wondered if this simple publication could be improved.

> "I did some research and found that, at the time, most calls to tradespeople were done by women. So my initial idea was to print woman-to-woman recommendations of good trades. I called it *Scout*. I had no investment money, so I just picked up the phone to my existing advertisers.

> "I told them the plan: 25,000 leaflets to be distributed in and around Chichester. If they wanted to be included, tradespeople had to provide six letters of recommendation from happy customers, plus insurance details and certifications. The plan was to publish quarterly."

# FIGHTING TO STAY AFLOAT

The response from directory advertisers was "fairly good", but cold calling was "hell". As a designer, Kevin took care of all the creative elements of the publication, but it was a real struggle just to claw in enough money to cover print and distribution costs.

He asked for £125 from each advertiser, a miserly sum given the extensive exposure. But this was an era before customer reviews of most kinds and people were sceptical. Then came a break, of sorts. Kevin was still freelancing as a graphic designer and one of his clients, a City worker based in London, became interested in the concept.

"I was very green as a businessman and I gave him 40% of the company. In return his wife agreed to hit the phones; she was a phenomenal saleswoman and we grew to five editions of *Scout*: the original and four new ones around southwest London.

"But we hit a bump in the road. The Scout Association found out about the name and they put lawyers onto us. I offered to change the name to *Scouted Out* but they continued the pressure, so I opted for *Trade Register*. This was around the year 2000 and we operated under the name for about 18 months."

Then, another snag. The dotcom boom was in full swing and Kevin sensed that the internet was a potential growth area. He investigated review sites "to copy", but discovered that there were none. This was the era before the likes of TripAdvisor, Square Meal, Airbnb, etc.

Undeterred, he called a meeting with his business partners. They disagreed with his assessment of a bright online future for reviews, arguing – partially correctly – that tradespeople would not accept being vetted and monitored so closely.

Kevin thought the ideal online product would feature case-by-case customer reviews, going on the basis that a tradesperson is only as good as their last job. The internet was the perfect facilitator – and yet he couldn't convince his co-owners of the concept.

"I consulted a trusted friend. They told me to hand the business over and start again. I had worked on it for two years, but after some thought I realised he was right. I gave them the four directories and kept my original. I didn't sell, I just gave them up."

Kevin then founded Vetted Ltd and began trading under the name Check A Trade. He spread the business focus into neighbouring Littlehampton and the tradespeople stayed loyal despite all the name changes. He was ready to go again.

"I told people I was introducing monitoring. Oh man! The guys who were with me were OK, but cold calling was miserable. The stock response was 'who the hell are you to monitor me?'. No one else was doing this so I had no competition and yet it was just so hard.

"Everything moved slowly. I was trying to introduce the trades to an entirely new culture and, although there was growth, I felt like I was just bumbling along the bottom not making any real progress. I took on a few staff members, but life was still tough."

# THE STRUGGLE AGAINST SELF DOUBT

Business continued like this until 2008, when Kevin had an epiphany. A friend lent him a set of spoken-word CDs called 'Awakening the Great Multitude Mind' by an American Christian motivational speaker. A devout Christian himself, Kevin devoured the lessons contained in the series.

The central message was about the nature of success. The speaker said his Christian values impeded his rise because he misinterpreted Bible teachings of being humble, meek and mild. They flew in the face of enterprise, he thought, in which the gospel is to become rich, powerful and influential.

"I realised he was talking about me. I would be embarrassed to arrive at church driving a new BMW or live in a five-bedroom detached house. But this was the wrong way to look at it – how could the Good Samaritan help anyone if he was poor too?

"There are more stories in the Bible about money than there are about Heaven and Hell, but you don't often hear them preached in churches. My whole attitude changed. I immediately started taking more risks, making important changes and understanding that my company could only get as big as I wanted it to get. I changed my job title to CEO."

Under the new regime, Kevin became wildly ambitious. He knew that people's actions, behaviour and achievements stem from their expectations. If you think small, that's what you will be. Changing this perception was the first step on the path to success.

He bought large maps of Great Britain and pinned them on the walls. His new domain: not local but national. It didn't seem plausible, but he now knew it was possible. He wrote down the sentence repeatedly: *I am going to be national.*

He discovered that a positive mental attitude impacted the morale of people around you. The mindset was infectious and the wheels started to turn. From the moment the tornado struck Selsey in 1998 to the 2008 turning point, the embryonic Checkatrade recruited four people. In the second decade of growth the figure was 330.

# RETURN ON INVESTMENT

It helped that public awareness about rogue traders had evolved, mainly due to new TV shows that trapped and outed charlatans. But, even so, the growing team had to work hard to establish the business as a first port of call for consumers.

"I realised we needed to build our profile and bring more people to the website and directories. But I didn't want to borrow money or take on a new partner, so the only option was to work with existing cash flow. This was tough, but I was a risk-taker now."

Kevin phoned local radio stations and proposed a swap deal: they would provide £1,000-worth of advertising in exchange for the back cover of the local Checkatrade directory. Some declined the offer, but others accepted it.

Without spending any money, the business was becoming known at the neighbourhood level. But this was no time to stand still; Kevin's new outlook on business meant he had to keep progressing.

> "In 2010, I phoned ITV and I asked how much it would cost for the smallest ad campaign possible. They put me in touch with the Thames Valley region, the tiniest in the network, who said it would cost £10,000. The next step was sponsoring the regional weather on Meridian, which cost £45,000 for three months.

> "It took four months to get the money together, but it was really successful and it turned us into a household name across the south of England. It paid for itself. When I was weighing up the move I asked my finance manager – also my niece – if we could afford it. She said 'no'. I asked if we could pay for the first month. She said 'just', so we did it anyway. That's how we built the company."

The next step was gigantic. A £1.1m campaign to sponsor the weather on *Good Morning Britain*. It was a 12-month contract and Checkatrade had funds available for the first month. Again, they rolled the dice on a speedy financial return. That was in 2013 and, five years later, the company still advertises in the same place.

# FAST GROWTH ONLINE

While Checkatrade was climbing up the rungs of national media exposure, it was also investing heavily in expanding its web offering. This began when the directories started to sell out. Tradespeople late to the party asked if they could have an online-only presence.

In the beginning, the website was basic, essentially a repository of files containing digital versions of the paper directories. But gradually the offline-online split shifted, starting at 100% directory and 0% online, moving to 100% online with 35% of these trades also featured in directories.

> "There was no magic wand, just a gradual movement online. We found it was a lot easier selling print to web users than it was the other way around."

After a hesitant start, Kevin describes growth as "pretty much solid" from the point at which he decided it was time to shift gears. His personal experience changed, too, from frustration and despair to a succession of great experiences.

He has enjoyed all the trappings of being the top dog, including running with the Olympic Torch in 2012 and handing over the Checkatrade Trophy at Wembley to the winners of the football league knockout tournament.

Another highlight was hitting £1m in turnover, an important psychological milestone for any ambitious business. The company multiplied this figure 23 times by the time HomeServe acquired it in two stages in 2017.

> "I parted with my business partners at *Scout* on amicable terms and I have seen them since. But I can't help thinking they must regret the decision not to go with me online, particularly knowing that I sold the company for £78m."

Checkatrade hit the big time because of ambition, guts and impeccable timing. But there was one other important ingredient: Kevin Bryne has always seen money as a yardstick of success and not collateral with which to buy nice things. Despite his enormous windfall, he lives the same lifestyle he did before the sale.

Clearly, his business life has changed. He has begun investing in ambitious start-ups with real purpose – those that make the world a better place – and he has set up a charitable foundation worth more than £6m. He knows that doing good is an important driver for entrepreneurs, because it was the fuel that drove him forward too.

"The whole time I was motivated by one principle, to clear the UK of rogue traders who take advantage of others and to promote people who want to do good work, ending their careers with a long list of happy customers behind them. If you're in it for the money, you'll let your principles slip somewhere down the line and that's a recipe for disaster."

For Kevin, making money is no longer an evil, so long as it happens as a by-product of doing some good. The fact that he has spent 20 years eliminating businesses who think differently is testament to that.

# CONCLUSION

**A**s the real-life stories and tips from fellow trades businesses throughout this book show, people tend to prosper when they have passion and pride, as well as the skills required to do a good job.

But aside from these elements there is no 'special sauce' involved. You have to plan to grow, which means putting in some extra time outside your normal day-to-day projects in order to assess your market position, research various opportunities and create a strategy to transform your business. But, other than that, it's a simple question of working hard to transform your dreams into a reality.

If you can focus on a goal and put in place things that will make it happen, then there's every chance your ambitions will solidify quickly.

People grumbling that it's too hard should pause for a moment to consider the experiences of those who have gone before. Charlie Mullins is one of the world's most successful tradespeople, yet his business was built on an ambition to upgrade the reputation of plumbing services back in the 1980s. Pimlico Plumbers developed a code of practice that required staff to be smart, courteous and professional. It was this, more than anything else, that made the business what it is today. Often, it's the simple stuff that makes a big difference.

Wayne de Wet can pick and choose his customers because he garnered a reputation for fastidiousness and attention to detail. For him, a job isn't done until every last detail is in place and the customer is 100% happy. His refusal to set in stone start dates for future projects shows that, for him, there is no more important customer than the one he's working with.

Dave Green dragged his fencing company out of the doldrums and turned it into a prosperous venture by instilling staff with a sense of commitment and dedication. Today the business has a reputation for getting the job done – no fuss, no complaints, just problems solved.

There is nothing in these three examples that you can't copy. If there's a magic formula to winning as a trades business, then perhaps it's this: high quality work + customer care + good marketing (via channels like Checkatrade) = repeat custom and recommendations. There really isn't much more to it than that.

The hard part is to do it consistently and to scale your business as demand grows without compromising any of your foundational principles. And that's where this book comes in. Hopefully it has made the path to growth clearer and easier to follow.

If you are an ambitious tradesperson hoping to make a mark on the world and a positive contribution to your profession, I wish you luck for the future!

# WITH THANKS

# NOTES

# NOTES

# NOTES

# NOTES